CROSS-SHAPED LEADERSHIP
ON THE ROUGH AND TUMBLE OF PARISH PRACTICE

CROSS-SHAPED
LEADERSHIP
ON THE ROUGH AND TUMBLE OF PARISH PRACTICE

John A. Berntsen

THE
ALBAN
INSTITUTE

Herndon, Virginia
www.alban.org

The Alban Institute
2121 Cooperative Way, Suite 100
Herndon, VA 20171-5370

www.alban.org

See permission credits on page 139.

Cover art: *Clay Jars* by Kirsten Malcolm Berry, www.KirstenMalcolmBerry.com. (Inscription translation: But we have this treasure in clay jars so that it be made clear that this extraordinary power belongs to God and does not come from us.—2 Corinthians 4:7, NRSV.)

Cover design by Tobias Becker, Bird Box Design.

Library of Congress Cataloging-in-Publication Data
    Berntsen, John A.
    Cross-shaped leadership : on the rough and tumble of parish practice /
    John A. Berntsen. p. cm.
    Includes bibliographical references (p. xxx).
    ISBN 978-1-56699-375-3

    1. Christian leadership. 2. Jesus Christ—Crucifixion. 3. Suffering—
      Religious aspects—Christianity. I. Title.

    BV652.1.B47 2008

    253—dc22
                      2008036040

12   11   10   09   08   VG   1   2   3   4   5

To Mary Lynn, Matt, T.J., "Sparky," and "Lloyd,"
who wondered what was going on in the back room.

Don't ask.

And to the congregations of Shepherd of the Hills Lutheran Church,
Whitehall (Egypt), Pennsylvania; the former East Penn–Mahoning
Lutheran Parish, Lehighton, Pennsylvania; Grace Lutheran Church,
Macungie, Pennsylvania; and
Trinity Lutheran Church, Perkasie, Pennsylvania.

And to the Candidacy Committee of the Southeastern Pennsylvania
Synod of the Evangelical Lutheran Church in America.

20.00

119504

The bright day of Christian community dawns wherever the early morning mists of dreamy visions are lifting.

—DIETRICH BONHOEFFER[1]

The church is always God hung between two thieves.

—RONALD ROLHEISER[2]

TABLE OF CONTENTS

FOREWORD

Decades ago, as a junior faculty member at a divinity school, I had my first invitation to participate in the ordination of a former student. I arrived at the church at the same time as a very senior faculty colleague who was to be the preacher that afternoon. As we walked up the church's front steps, he growled, "Every time I have to preach at one of these ordinations, the only thing I can think to say is, 'May God have mercy on your soul.'"

My colleague was a person of faith and an excellent theologian. He hadn't become world-weary, cynical, or sardonic. He was simply being real—unsentimental and faithfully honest about the rough and tumble that is entailed by God's call to what John Berntsen terms the "public leadership of parish practice," the call that churches acknowledge and celebrate in their ordination services.

In this wonderfully clear-eyed book, Berntsen captures that same realism by inviting us to see public leadership in parish practice as what he calls a "cross-shaped" leadership. "Cross-shaped" might wrongly suggest that, while recognizably traditional, his take on church leadership will be abstractly and impractically doctrinal, off-puttingly grim, or at the very least piously "spiritual" but disengaged from the "real" world of church life. However, nothing could be further from the truth.

The term "cross-shaped" obviously gives a theological spin to the phrase "leadership of parish practice," but what makes it theological is neither abstract nor impractical. Rather, what makes it theological is concretely practical. It is no accident that Berntsen speaks not of leadership in the abstract, nor of "ordained leadership," but of "leadership of parish practice." To see why, consider the most elementary advice given to novice poets, short story writers, and novelists at writers' workshops: if you have something to say, show, don't tell. That advice applies even more to parishes: If you have good news you want to share, don't tell it to us by outlining it abstractly. Show it to us by the character of the concrete and particular practices that make up your common life. These practices define the community's particular identity: "who" it collectively is.

Christian parishes typically say that they are communities called by God through the crucified and resurrected Jesus to share good news—namely, the news that God has brought the entire human family into community with God through Jesus of Nazareth, crucified and raised from the dead. That is inescapably a theological definition of who they are. Accordingly, the practices that make up the communities' common life must be "cross-shaped" in order to faithfully and concretely show—not just abstractly tell—their good news. As the communities' definition is inescapably theological, so are the practices that make up their common life. That means that what is theological about parish practices is their very concreteness, and that is why any account of the "leadership of parish practices" must be a theological account from beginning to end.

By framing his book from the outset as an account of public leadership of parish practice as a "cross-shaped leadership," Berntsen has kept his account theological; and by focusing on the theological character of leadership of "parish practice" he has kept it concretely practical and tied to the particularities of the everyday world—avoiding the pitfall of being "abstractly and impractically doctrinal."

As for the suggestion that a "cross-shaped" account of public leadership of parish practice must end up being unbearably grim, you only have to read a couple of chapters to see how preposterous that is. This is often an engagingly funny book, sometimes laugh-out-loud funny. Obviously, there's nothing comic about crucifixion. However, three of the main things that "cross-shaped" practices do are shine a bright light on God's sense of humor (see the last chapter!), expose the absurdities of our own pretensions and self-delusions (it's called "judgment," and it begins at home), and deepen our own capacities to laugh at ourselves (that's a big part of repentance and conversion). So, too, as Berntsen repeatedly points out, leadership of such parish practices ought to have a heightened capacity to laugh heartily at its own pretensions and self-delusions about leadership skill, prominence, "success," and even "glory," just because it *is* "cross-shaped."

A sharper eye for one's own absurdities and an increased freedom to laugh at oneself are only two of the personal capacities that need to be cultivated in order to exercise a "cross-shaped" public leadership of parish practice. The traditional name for disciplined cultivation of such abilities is "spiritual discipline" or, more simply, "spirituality." This brings us to the suspicion that Berntsen's account of "cross-shaped" leadership of parish practice will be talk of ministerial leadership that is no doubt piously "spiritual" but is disengaged from the "real" world of church life. He explicitly rules that out, however, by stressing that the kind of leadership of parish practice he envisions is a *public* leadership in the "rough and tumble" of parish practice. Two "publics" overlap here: the smaller public consisting of a parish's common life and the public consisting of the larger common life of the time and place into which the parish is set. Both publics are arenas in which power is exercised toward various ends. In both, various kinds of power are unevenly distributed. Therefore both are arenas of the rough and tumble of disagreement, contestation, competition, and conflict. That is why my colleague felt called to pray for God's mercy on the souls of those called to exercise public leadership in parish practice. Berntsen is entirely clear about that reality. The power of his book lies in the way he shows (not tells!) how leadership of parish practice *in* that kind of "public" space can nevertheless really be "cross-shaped."

At the same time, it's obvious that the phrase "cross-shaped" does associate Berntsen's view of leadership of parish practice with traditions of Christian spiritual discipline that are often called "the way of the cross." Such disciplines aim to shape people's interiority or subjectivity. However, his point is that they aim to do so not to enable us to disengage from the public world but to engage it more freely and vigorously. Berntsen is particularly good at showing how public leadership of parish practice is liberated when it is formed by "cross-shaped" spiritual disciplines. It is liberated by being nurtured and energized when dispirited and worn out by the rough and tumble of parish practice. And it is liberated by learning to die to the absurd (if un-self-aware) pretensions and self-delusions that hamstring leadership of parish practice, especially the delusion that its calling is to help God out by fixing broken people and saving them on God's behalf. As Berntsen says in his last line, a truly cross-shaped understanding of leadership of parish practice challenges "the pious notion that God somehow 'needs' our vocation. It's the neighbor who does. God's doing just fine."

If you are one whose vocation is to exercise public leadership in the rough and tumble of parish practice, John Berntsen's wise book may be God's mercy on your soul.

DAVID H. KELSEY
Weigle Professor Emeritus of Theology
Yale Divinity School

ACKNOWLEDGMENTS

I'm deeply grateful to the following people who encouraged me in this project and were willing to give me their constructive criticism about both the content and the form of the writing: Professor David Kelsey of Yale, my former teacher, who read the whole of it and encouraged me to persist in spite of the slings and arrows of the publishing world; Professor Timothy J. Wengert of the Lutheran Theological Seminary at Philadelphia, who allowed me to pester him unceasingly about the Lutheran bona fides of my most eccentric ideas; Professor Donald Capps of Princeton, who on principle doesn't use e-mail, but answered my every phone call and snail-mail inquiry about humor and religion, a subject on which his knowledge is encyclopedic; neighbor and friend, economics Professor Jim Dearden of Lehigh University, and Dr. Dennis O'Hara, clinical psychologist of Physis Associates of West Chester, Pennsylvania, both of whom helped me understand how those who are not religious fanatics and church cult insiders might get lost amid my theological pretensions (Dennis was also the one who urged me to become acquainted with the timeless work of Karen Horney); Pastor D. Craig Landis, dearest friend, who not only read my rantings, but also helped me curb the worst of my narcissism; and most of all my editors, Beth Gaede and Jean Caffey Lyles, who always told me the truth in love, whether I wanted to hear it or not. A good book is never written; it's edited.

Finally, my thanks, love, and fervent prayers for healing go to Dr. Conrad Weiser, clinician extraordinaire of church professionals, bishops, seminarians, and congregations throughout the United States. Bill's fierce love taught me, and has taught countless others, always to find God "under the form of the opposite," and always, always to "say what a thing actually is."

INTRODUCTION

The cross has a way of intruding itself into your life. Often knowledge of the cross goes hand in hand with the experience of some significant life failures. To recognize that you are, after all, a broken vessel can sober you up a bit about your quest for glory.

In our culture the quest for "glory," and so the failure to achieve it, wears many faces. The recent cult of celebrity seduces many of us, and not least those who crave the food of endless attention, praise, and adoration. The neurotic need for order and security beckons those whose quest is for an ultimate "safety" that the world cannot give short of the grave (the only place where everything is in order is a cemetery). And many cannot live their lives except *through* others and with their approval (prompting the old twelve-step joke about the person on her deathbed who saw someone else's life flash before her).

We are loath to acknowledge any of this, of course. We have become practiced at "keeping our game face on" and "never letting them see you sweat"—unless it's to make a spectacle of our woes by turning life into another second-rate "reality show." Perhaps the starkest reality is being "useless" amid a global marketplace whose mythology is that you can "be all that you can be" if only you will "reinvent" yourself daily. As the social scientist Richard Sennett reminds us, "Failure is the great modern taboo."[1] In America, it is "our unmentionable subject."[2]

This book is an essay on the vocation of the leader. It is a theology of the vocation of leadership for parish practice. It is written from the standpoint of what Christians call theology of the cross.

Theology of the cross is not a theory that explains anything. It is knowing God in the midst of suffering and brokenness and creaturely limitation. Theology of the cross is an experience, and it ceases to be theology of the cross when it becomes an explanation or an analysis of something, such as "why bad things happen to good people." We can do only one of two things about the cross: flee it or die on it—and if the latter, then when we have been raised up, we can proclaim the cross, so that it does its saving work.

Of course the cross is an event in history. But it is also an event in the daily life of believers. In other words, the cross happened not only in 29 CE in ancient Palestine; it happens also in the event of proclamation and in faith. Though unrepeatable on the stage of history, the cross repeats itself in the community's worship and in the ministry of its faith active in works of love.

In this book the cross is about more than the crucifixion on Good Friday. Speaking of the cross is really shorthand for the whole drama of salvation. The cross is God's decisive act of reconciling the world to God. *The cross is about dying and rising with Christ.* It is about what we undergo, and therefore what we lose and gain, in this dying and rising. The cross is about the death of our old self, the self born of Adam and Eve, and the rising up of a new self born of "the Spirit of him who raised Jesus from the dead" (Rom. 8:11).

At a deeper level, the cross is the story of the world's resistance to grace. The cross is the showdown, yes, the confrontation, between a steadfastly loving God who wills and calls a world into covenant partnership (all humanity is *co*-humanity, as the theologian Karl Barth would put it) and a world that wants to live in its own strength playing God for itself. Jesus comes preaching a kingdom of righteousness, justice, and unconditional love; and the world says, "No, thanks. We think our system of merit and scorekeeping and judgment is safer. We prefer the reign of our marketplace to your upside-down kingdom that reckons by grace. So count us out."

Those who lead are subject to the cross no less than others. Public leadership in the church is subject to death and resurrection. The very initiatives, actions, and plans of leaders *undergo* the cross. Helpfully, Martin Luther refers to the daily life of believers in terms of "the doings of the saints." Taking his lead, in the pages ahead we will be looking at the "doings" of ministry as subject to, as "suffering," the event of the cross. Under the cross, ministry dies to itself and rises anew.

The face of one pastoral candidate comes before me as we begin. Like so many candidates these days (though the trends keep changing), he was second-career, in this case a former mortgage banker. Let's call him Dan. Dan's marriage was ending just as he entered seminary and the church's discernment process. One can only describe Dan as "willful." He often said that he "*had to be* a pastor." He also "had to be" and "had to do" many other things. Finally, on a walk during a retreat, I said to him, "Dan, if you *have to be* a pastor, you're not ready for it." And then I found myself asking, "When are you going to let yourself die?"

Eventually, Dan's seemingly impenetrable defenses crumbled. Perhaps it was the numerous "no's" and "not yets" that he heard from the church about his readiness for public ministry. Fortunately for him and for our church, there was a breakthrough, and today Dan is an effective working pastor. I want to believe that his willfulness was met at the cross: that something in him—namely, his old self—died, and that a new self was being raised up.

The cross is God's agent in the voyage of vocational self-discovery. It may lead us out of public ministry as well as into it. One of my resident advisors from college was what we call a "pipeliner," a student on a straight track from undergraduate school to the seminary. After many years, I lost track of his whereabouts, but I noticed that his name no longer appeared on the national clergy roster of my denomination. Curious, I began to search the Internet (aka "the font of truth"), only to discover that he had gone into business as a "dog musher." I am not making this up. There is indeed such a profession, as I then learned. Dog mushers raise and train sled dogs for use in northern climates. My friend had left professional ministry and taken up commercial dog mushing.

He owns a small business in northern Minnesota that caters to tourists and outdoor adventurers. Whether he has ever raced in the Iditarod, I don't know. But you can go to his website and see a beautiful color photograph of him cheek by jowl with one of his beloved huskies. When I wrote to him and asked what had happened, he responded laconically, "It's a long story." The path he took to what is, I hope, his true self was obviously a frosty one.

Just as those in my tradition like to echo Martin Luther's use of the word "daily" when it comes to baptism, so the moment-by-moment doings of ministry are subject to countless deaths and resurrections, few of which are heroic or glorious. The aim of this book is to explore how this transformation takes place amid the rough-and-tumble of parish practice. The pages ahead are an exploration of what I call *cross-shaped leadership.* Each chapter is an essay about one facet of cross-shaped leadership.

First, cross-shaped leadership is not only about taking an initiative but also about *receiving the initiative of others*—the divine Other and the others of the world. Here we will look at ministry in terms of *what leaders undergo,* rather than what they *do.* Leadership is about what I like to call *action in passion.* The very act of leading is subject to or "suffers" the event of the Word's proclamation and the world's resistance to that proclamation. Leadership is caught up in, and so is *a response to,* the undergoing of this event. In practice this means that what leaders do is always provisional, contextual, and fallible. It is always interim in nature.

Second, the struggle within us between the true self and the false self is the root of vocational discernment and ministry formation. Rediscovering our true self is the central challenge of the Christian life and identity. The challenges of leadership magnify the vulnerability of the self in its true and false guises.

Third, humility marks cross-shaped leadership. There's not much humility in evidence among today's heralded "visionary" or "purpose-driven" leaders. Yet strong-willed humility (a paradox, of course!) is the most noticeable mark on leaders left by the cross.

Fourth, cross-shaped leaders are focused on people before ideas, answers, or master plans. They are listeners and questioners before they are visionaries or seers. Cross-shaped leaders focus first on the Who of God and the who of the people in covenant, and only secondly on the what of the leader's supposed vision. Biblically, vision arises from, and remains grounded in, *a community of people in partnership or covenant.* Vision is always responsive; it is a function of the call and response of a living dialogue. Otherwise, as so often in institutional life, when vision becomes detached from partnerships and covenants (spoken or unspoken), it deteriorates into an ideology or an agenda. It hardens into an abstraction, and then it commands by coercion instead of willing obedience.

Fifth, cross-shaped leaders live a double life. Every group has its stated mission for work and an unspoken, usually unconscious, emotional contract about why people have come together. Leadership is a dance: it always means getting on with the mission at the same time that one tends to the unconscious life and health of the body. Ministry is always "in sickness and in health." It means befriending the imperfect and sometimes the irrational. Moreover, our life together under God's Word calls for mutual love and discipline of one another as members of the assembly. In this regard, the clinical/health model of community life ("healthy vs. unhealthy" congregations) is rooted and grounded in what the confessional tradition calls the "marks of the church," such as the Office of the Keys, the Offices of Ministry, and so forth.

Sixth, humor is a sign of our need for grace. Cross-shaped leaders take themselves less seriously, because they take God's grace more seriously. Laughter, with its recognition of the contradictions that make up our life together, can keep us honest about our allotted place as creatures and even call us to that repentance, to that change of mind and heart, which prepares us to hear once again the good news of God's forgiveness and unconditional love.

Three sources feed the reflections in the pages ahead: (1) some thirty years in parish ministry, most of it as an "afterpastor," one who comes after a time of conflict, trauma, or misconduct in a congregation; (2) ten years of work in what my Lutheran denomination calls candidacy, which is the formation and screening process for pastors and church workers; and (3) my own lifelong struggle trying to discover "what I want to be when I grow up."

MADE BY THE CROSS
Undergoing Jesus

The cross is an event . . . The cross is the doing of God to us.
—Gerhard Forde[1]

Undergoing Jesus must be the center of any Christian spirituality.
—Ronald Rolheiser[2]

*Jesus does not fulfill his vocation in action only but also
in passion. He doesn't just fulfill his vocation by doing things . . .
but also by letting things be done to him . . . by receiving other
people's initiatives.* —Henri J. M. Nouwen[3]

*One of two things must necessarily follow when we rely on our own
watchfulness: either arrogance or worry.* —Martin Luther[4]

What does "the message about the cross" (1 Cor. 1:18) have to do with leadership in the church? How does the cross story shape the vocation, the everyday life and mission, of the leader? What is cross-shaped leadership?

We may speak passionately about "theology of the cross" in a seminary classroom or at a conference of church professionals. For instance, we may admonish one another about the centrality of the cross in preaching. We may even have a lively awareness of the cross in the deeply personal settings of pastoral care. The hidden place where we are all but certain to know the cross, however, is in our own lives. There we don't talk *about* it; we *undergo* it. This turn to "undergoing," to what both we and our ministry endeavors "suffer," is the key to any deeper insight into Christian vocation. Cross-shaped leadership is the *public* face of such vocation amid the Christian assembly in the world.

Ministry is hard. Ministry is, in fact, impossible. This is perhaps the worst-kept secret in the life of the church. Just try to referee a fair fight about the virtues of "contemporary" versus "traditional" worship. Now *there's* a party. It's a perfect storm in which leaders are pressured either to pick winners and losers, or to feed the multitudes by offering a cafeteria of consumer choices.

Or try to respond appropriately to the man who once complained that I had failed to visit him in the hospital—it turned out that he had deliberately withheld his name from the chaplain's office. He said, "If I had told you I was in the hospital, you would have *had to come* and see me, and it wouldn't have counted."

Or consider the newly minted leader's foundering upon the hard reality of all groups, including the Christian assembly, that operate on two levels at once: that of the stated work, task, or mission; and that of primitive unconscious desires, fears, and needs that may morph into the *real*, though unspoken, mission. The assembly may have its well-crafted mission statement, for instance, and the council and call committee may have a whiz-bang of a strategic plan and job description for the staff, but then the real, or operative, job description lurks in the shadows of the congregation's collective soul.

It might go something like this: *the job of the staff is to take care of the people, and the job of the people is to be taken care of by the staff.* In this case, dependency is the unspoken contract or covenant about why people are gathered here in the first place. If this hidden contract remains unfulfilled, unacknowledged, or left in the shadows, then the stated mission of proclaiming the gospel, reaching out to the community, and working for justice and peace will become stuck in a molasses of foot-dragging and grudging go-along-to-get-along compliance. Cross-shaped leadership, therefore, is often about breaking old contracts and making new covenants, and it's about accepting the irrational as a force to be reckoned with in the process.

Here's the good news, though. Once we've accepted the truth that ministry is hard, even impossible—once we've stopped living in denial of this reality, or perhaps whining about it—it becomes the truth that sets us free. We cease being gloomy servants, weighed down by our resentful conviction that we are all alone in our work—the closet atheism (see chapter 4) born of the worry, "If I don't do it, nobody will"—and instead become joyful co-workers of a strong, wise, and consoling Lord.

Much if not most of the grief in ministry comes from the fantasy that there ought to be some glory in it. Surely our ministry ought to count for something. After all, aren't we "saving souls"? (Well, no, we're not. Jesus does all the saving.) Glory here doesn't just mean attention, adoration, and credit. True, to fill a void in ourselves, some of us hanker after all this. Count me among them.

"Glory," however, also means that we enter public ministry, even if unawares, to lift ourselves above our personal woundedness, or to find a refuge from the storms of life. The ranks of the clergy are thickly populated with those enacting unconscious life strategies to compensate for the self's early childhood experience of some perceived or real deprivation (see chapter 2). No doubt "wounded healers," as famously depicted by Henri Nouwen, are a noble band of believers. All too often, however, leaders may end up being what, in informal conversation, Father Nouwen used to call "wounded wounders." As a colleague recently said to me, "It's great to be a 'wounded healer,' as long as you're not still bleeding!" In the same vein, the pastor, psychologist, and church-vocations clinician Conrad Weiser aptly describes many church professionals as "healers, harmed and harmful."[5]

The Cross: The Doing of God to Us

I first began to think more seriously about these matters when home recuperating from an operation. Flat on my back and unable to speak and eat without severe pain from throat surgery, I finally picked up Gerhard Forde's *On Being a Theologian of the Cross.* The book had been sitting unread and gathering dust for months, ever since I had heard author and keynote speaker Marva Dawn recommend the title as "must reading."

Old friends who had studied with Forde had spoken of him as very much a theological original whose sometimes curmudgeonly slant on matters had a way of exposing religious superficialities. What I thought would be simply a "good read" accruing to my continuing education, or at least to my entertainment, turned out to be an intense look in the mirror of my professional and personal life.

What can one say about the severe wisdom of Forde's writing except that it's a kind of tonic for a church that has lost its gospel nerve? Ostensibly an academic exercise in interpreting Martin Luther's Heidelberg Disputation of 1518—a document considered key to Luther's early thought, especially his theology of the cross—it is in reality a commentary on the illusions at the heart of much contemporary theology, spirituality, and ministry practice. Forde reminds us that the cross is above all an event, a happening that confronts and undoes us. "The cross is an event. . . . The cross is the doing of God to us."[6]

In Forde's often barbed commentary, the cross is not only the narrative of Jesus's passion as told in Matthew, Mark, Luke, and John. As witnessed to by these very accounts, the cross is God's frontal assault on the world's determination to be its own god. What the cross reveals is that we—all of us—do not really want to "let God be God." Why? Because then we would have to do the one thing we humans find most difficult: *trust*. To let God be God frightens us, because it means dying to life's central illusion: *control*. As we stand before God, the illusion of control is our drug of choice, and the cross works on us to expose its lie.

Reformation historian Timothy Wengert makes sure we don't drift into misty abstraction about the cross when he insists that it is above all an *experienced* reality in which our bones are stretched out in the agony of personal loss.[7] Theology of the cross is not a religious theory that helps explain from a safe distance God's nature and ways. Rather, the cross is the God of Jesus in the Spirit *happening to us*. It is the undoing, the death, of our human god-illusion. As such, it is God calling us to embrace our humanness by dying and rising with Christ. "We are meant to be human beings, not divine," Martin Luther says in his devotional writings.[8] Cross-shaped leaders, to say nothing of Christian people at large, would do well to make this their mission statement.

The cross, then, Forde reminds us, reveals our resistance to grace. It is what "must" happen (Luke's Gospel constantly speaks of the "must," the inevitability, of the passion: Luke 9:22; 13:33; 21:9; 22:37; 24:7; 24:44) when our every breath and action go into the god-project our lives seem bent on constructing. The cross cuts to the quick because it exposes our chronic mistrust that God has done all the saving there is to be done. "Must Jesus bear the cross alone?" the old hymn asks. The answer is yes, so long as we insist on being in godlike control of our creaturely destiny.

The very narrative flow of the Bible exhibits this cross-shaped encounter of God's grace with human willfulness. Students of the Scriptures have often noticed that the Gospel accounts are "passion stories with long introductions." Even from birth, the whole of Jesus's story is overcast by the final journey to Jerusalem and the shadow of Holy Week. Just check out bad old King Herod the Great's plotting and evildoing in Matthew's Christmas story (Matt. 2). Or shudder as you read about John the Baptist's fate under Herod Antipas, or as I like to call him, "Herod, Jr." (Mark 6:14–29). Passion predictions also frame the visionary glimpse of glory (really, a glimpse of Easter) on the Mount of Transfiguration (Matt. 17; Mark 9; Luke 9). Long before the entrance into Jerusalem on Palm Sunday, Jesus already undergoes the passion.

Responsive Leadership: "Action in Passion"

What does this all-pervading reality of the passion in the gospels have to do with the question of vocation? How does it help us articulate Jesus's calling and the calling of those who minister and lead in his name?

The spiritual writers W. H. Vanstone and Henri Nouwen point out that in the first half of the Gospel accounts, Jesus seems to be a "man of action." He goes here. He goes there. He preaches. He heals. He speaks parables. He breaks into people's lives, appearing and disappearing with suddenness. Readers have long noted that Mark's story of Jesus is especially abrupt and fast-paced. Moreover, Jesus's early ministry in Galilee seems to have been the place and time of his greatest human popularity.

But then, from the midpoint of the Gospels onward (roughly, from the Transfiguration), others increasingly do things *to* Jesus.

More and more, Jesus is acted *upon*. He is challenged and argued with. He is plotted against. His popularity arouses resentment and hostility. He becomes, as Vanstone and Nouwen note, the object of other people's initiatives—initiatives that betray a misunderstanding of what it means to be the Messiah. At least humanly, Jesus seems more passive. (We get "passive" and "passion" from the Latin *passio*.) He *undergoes*, that is, he "suffers," more and more at human hands.[9] Read Mark's account of the passion, and note the length of Jesus's statements and responses as the action unfolds. The sentences grow shorter and shorter until we hear Jesus respond to Pilate at the trial, "You say so" (Mark 15:2). Ultimately, the gospel reveals that it is not human hands alone that have been at work. To borrow a phrase from the theologian Reinhard Hutter, Jesus is "suffering divine things."[10]

What we rarely speak about in public ministry, or for that matter ministry in daily life, is that, like Jesus himself, we fulfill our calling not only in what we make happen, but also in *what we undergo*, what we "suffer." In what is arguably his most programmatic statement on Christian vocation, Henri Nouwen declares, "Jesus does not fulfill his vocation in action only but also in passion. He doesn't just fulfill his vocation by doing things the Father sent him to do, but also by letting things be done to him that the Father allows to be done to him, by receiving other people's initiatives."[11]

How can we escape this "paschal mystery" at the heart of the gospel that *Jesus fulfills his vocation, his calling, not only in action but also in passion*? How can this not in some way be true as well for us, who serve and lead in his name? Beyond stammering, however, what can we say about such leadership? Can there be leadership in passion, what I have come to call *action in passion*? How does ministry that "suffers" divine things work in practice?

As I hope we will see in the pages ahead, this kind of leadership is first and foremost *responsive leadership*. In contrast with the current fashion for "visionary" or "purpose-driven" leaders, cross-shaped leaders are not primarily the providers of master plans, nor are they master builders. Because all of ministry is shaped by what it "suffers," because it is always dying to itself and rising anew, it bears these marks: it is provisional, contextual, and fallible. Cruciform ministry is open-ended and has the character of a pilot project. It is always under construction and revision.

Take preaching. By lunchtime on Sunday, if the sermon is worth its salt, it should be different from what it was at the beginning of the week. And it will be different even from what it was the moment you walked into the church building on Sunday. If you're lucky, you may have had more than one whack at its delivery, so that you can say what you really meant to say to begin with. Proclamation is always a work in progress, an unfolding event, because of its very nature: it is caught up in the living, and so *unfinished*, dialogue between the Word and the world. This dialogue is one of call and response in real time, and it never happens apart from a gathered community. Thus, the church's preaching voice can only be responsive. Moreover, caught up as it is in the living dialogue of the Word with the world, preaching meets the world's resistance to the gospel of grace by its witness to, and confession of, the truth of God's reign. Martin Luther insists that the cross cannot be separated from the act of its preaching: "So if Christ were crucified a hundred times in a day and no one preached it, then the forgiveness of sins would be lost. For this reason the work completed on the cross must be contained in the Word and offered to people through the Word."[12] Preaching takes on the character of an offering, a sacrifice of praise. It is both confessional and liturgical. It responds to what it "suffers" under the event of the Word.

One of my favorite Sunday-night church services on television comes from an urban black congregation in which the preacher has standing next to him in the pulpit an assistant called "the reader." While the pastor preaches, "the reader" browses through the Bible, seemingly at random, to find supporting, questioning, or supplementary texts with which he interrupts the preacher in a rhythmic give-and-take. Rhetorically, the call and response of proclamation unfolds as a three-way interplay within the assembly.

The recent emphasis in some churches on clergy health and wellness is another illustration of the fallible character of cross-shaped ministry. Some of us are better than others at self-care: taking our day off and vacation and making time for family, exercise, and spiritual disciplines. The simple fact that we have

observed these "boundaries" outwardly or in keeping with the letter of professional conduct does not mean that we have internal-
ized them or taken them to heart. But better outwardly than not
at all, of course.

Once I interviewed with a call committee whose members spoke
glibly about the so-called work/life balance (a current management cliché) the congregation's staff had achieved in the aftermath
of the previous senior pastor's workaholic tenure. I marveled that
twenty-five years could be overcome so quickly in a congregation
shaped by its leader. Balance, indeed. As any person in recovery will
attest, self-care is a never-ending journey filled with the pitfalls of
self-deception and frequent relapse. Precisely because our addictions are so cunning in their lies, and thus the ministry of self-care
so humanly fallible, we learn not only to "take one day at a time,"
but more radically to heed the call of the cross to "die every day"
(1 Cor. 15:31) to our old, egocentric self.

Earthly Suffering and Heavenly Suffering

Given our frequent use of words like "passion," "suffers," and
"undergoes," it's urgent to pause here and ask how our passion is like and how it is *not* like Jesus's passion. What does "passion" mean for us, and what does it, and *can* it, *not* mean?

Martin Luther was adamant that our suffering is an earthly
matter, while only Christ's suffering is heavenly and makes the
world righteous. Preaching on Good Friday morning, March 26,
1529, about Jesus in the Garden of Gethsemane, Luther exhorted,
"Do not allow yourself to be seduced and mix your suffering and
Christ's suffering together!"[13] Our suffering may serve "to improve
things on earth and to spread the gospel more and more."[14] At
times it may even serve as "a work to mortify your flesh."[15] (It may
help tame and discipline our human nature in its self-centered-
ness.) But what our suffering absolutely cannot do is to atone for
one sin. Our suffering doesn't "earn" anything before God, even
though a parishioner may say, as I have sometimes had it said to
me in bitter jest, "Pastor, I know I'm going to heaven, because I've
had my hell on earth." (The spouse often agrees.)

In his full humanity, Christ is one with us in the anguish of our suffering, and this presence is deeply consoling. Moreover, our human suffering is both a call and, often, *the result* of a call for us to "bear one another's burdens" (Gal. 6:2). But in his divinity, only Christ's suffering saves and redeems. To imagine otherwise is both to dishonor Christ and to crush the believer under an unbearable weight.

This is truly good news for those in ministry. It means that while we are called to be "little christs," as the popular Christian apologist C. S. Lewis liked to put it, we die to the illusion that we are in any way the original Christ—that anything we do saves or redeems.[16] When we understand ministry initiatives as always dying to themselves, and thus as action in passion, then we cease to labor under the illusion of rescuing the world or its inhabitants. We renounce being highly trained, though poorly paid, enablers and saviors.

The theological background here is Martin Luther's recognition that the gospel of salvation is a matter of what he calls the "passive righteousness" of faith.[17] Passive righteousness means that when it comes to salvation we are complete and utter receivers. As humans account "doing," there is absolutely nothing to do. We are literally passive . . . when it comes to salvation. We undergo it. We "suffer" it. It comes down from heaven and, as the Reformers liked to say, it is "imputed" to us.

What then of the doings of our lives and of our varied ministries? Are we left with some kind of weird, mystical "do-nothing-ism"? Luther responds by making a sharp distinction between that which is "above us" and that which is "beneath us,"[18] and even more definitively he insists that the "passive righteousness" of faith calls for the earthly response of our "active righteousness." The "two kinds of righteousness," passive and active, must always be carefully distinguished, and never the twain shall meet . . . except as a heavenly call that evokes an earthly response.[19] This distinction is truly liberating not only for theology but also for ministry. We have free will and free choice with regard to those things that are "beneath us," that is, our wills are free when it comes to our ordinary earthly affairs. We can decide where to live, what to have for lunch, what to do for work, where to go on vacation, whom to marry, what style of clothes to wear, what books to read, what teams to root for, what party to vote for, what charities to support, what service to render, and all the rest. This is our active, earthly righteousness, which in no way saves, yet is a grateful response to the free gift of salvation.

But our wills are not free; in fact they are captive, when it comes to the heavenly business of salvation. Why captive? Simply because salvation is a "done deal" in Jesus's death and resurrection; it's a *finished work* before we are even a twinkle in our parents' eyes. We contribute exactly zero to it. We are literally passive. Moreover, given our chronic human suspicion of this "deal that sounds too good to be true," our human track record reveals that we *habitually do not trust such an offer*. We are "*bound* and determined" (hence the much misunderstood notion of the "bondage of the will") to want to save ourselves. Like addicts, we cannot help ourselves. In the language of the daytime talk shows, we have "control issues." Only at the cross does this willfulness of the creature meet its end.

Trusting that the affairs of heaven are a finished work (passive righteousness), however, we creatures are liberated from having to make a god-project out of our earthly lives and ministry. The cross sends us back into our everyday life free to labor within its down-to-earth confines and unreservedly to serve the bodily and earthly needs of our neighbor (active righteousness). As action in passion (an active response to what has been passively—that is, trustingly—received!), our varied ministries die to the pretension that they can, or should, save anything or anybody.

Yet in this very dying, our efforts become less anxious and more open to a broader, more spacious field of ministry endeavor. The expanse of all creation and history is opened up for service. By no longer pretending to play God, and thus vainly attempting to fix the affairs of *both* heaven and earth, we are free to do justice to our work on earth. This is the true meaning of servant leadership.

God's Masks: Doing What Is Immediately to Hand

It should start to become clearer now that when we understand vocation, ministry, and leadership as action in passion—that is, as shaped by what they "suffer" or die to under faith's passive righteousness—they often take on a very earthly, even common-place, appearance or guise. Not only are the doings of ministry always provisional and fallible, but they also are always contextual; they are bound to a here-and-now place. Ministry and leadership do not float up in the air.

Martin Luther had a rather homely, domestic way of putting this. He spoke of the "doings of the saints" as the responsibilities of a household for which someone has oversight. The commonplace duties of the household of faith may not appear to be overtly "religious." They are, however, "the work of the Lord our God under a mask."[20] As I have said above, the cross redirects our gaze and works back into the earthly realm, giving us a renewed relationship to history, creation, and even space and time. The practical result is that the cross calls us to trust that even the most routine duties and demands of ministry (who says that calling the plumber is beneath the dignity of the senior pastor?) are "the masks" concealing God at work. This radical trust carries several implications for ministry practice and leadership.

One, learn the wisdom of "bloom and grow where you are planted." When church workers become restless in their call or assignment, wise mentors may urge us to consider "growing in place" (as more than one bishop has said to me) rather than exiting the present ministry setting in a fight-or-flight panic. In lieu of a "grass-is-greener" comparison-shopping approach to our discernment process, the cross sends us back into our present context to probe it in greater depth. The aim of the cross is not to keep us as church workers "down on the farm," but rather to renew our sense of vocation itself. The cross calls us to become unstuck from how we approach ministry, whatever its particular setting. We may go or we may stay, but the cross will not allow us to stay the same.

Again, Luther has an almost domestic way of making this point. He speaks of doing "what is immediately to hand."[21] "Go eat your bread with enjoyment, and drink your wine with a merry heart . . . Whatever your hand finds to do, do with all your might."[22] Get over thinking that to determine your priorities and to know with certainty where your actions will lead, as if that were even humanly possible, you must have a master plan for the progress of the world! Yet doing "what is immediately at hand" hardly means that the on-site leader should operate without working priorities or a sense of what tasks most clearly define her ministry office. Rather, it means that what the leader is truly called to do is *not to be found in some place*, such as "over there," other than where she finds herself.

Two, beware of the lure of "specialization." (In ministry, beware of anything that ends with the pretentious suffix of "ization." There's always less to it than meets the eye.) It's tempting to ask, in what kinds of work do cross-shaped leaders "specialize"? Because of the emotional tone surrounding the language of suffering and the cross, we might imagine that ministry in its wake is something of extraordinary expertise or spiritual valor. Perhaps there is a unique set of activities that make up the workday of cross-shaped leaders. Maybe they are particularly empathic and sensitive to the needs and suffering of others. Maybe they engage in martyrlike deeds. Perhaps they have highly specialized training, and even licensure, in some field outside basic parish practice. One pictures a kind of elite Special Forces group of spiritual commandos; indeed, "soldiers of the cross."

When I attended seminary, it was popular to advise that if you were going to be, say, a pastor, it was only prudent to have a second field of professional expertise such as law, or counseling, or business administration, or whatever. Supposedly, this "dual competency," as it was called, might give you more credibility and impact in the real world. There was a certain loss of nerve about being a plain old pastor, minister, or church worker. As a result, the call to find, and then ground, one's ministry in what is "immediately at hand" goes unheard. Ministry becomes detached from its contextual foundation.

To the casual observer, then, there may in fact be nothing "special" about what leaders of the cross regularly do, if by special we mean a set of ministry activities or programs that are uniquely "religious" or mystical or intrinsically redemptive in their nature. Because the cross has taken out of our hands the business of heaven and its salvation, we are called to trust that God disguises God's work behind the "masks" that are the makeup of our ordinary earthly life.

Three, "paying the rent" is fully worthy of our best efforts. The influential church consultant Lyle Schaller popularized the phrase "paying the rent," coined by James D. Glasse, the late president of Lancaster Theological Seminary.[23] Schaller and Glasse observe that when leaders are faithful to basic ministry functions like preaching, teaching, visiting, and a modicum of parish organizing/planning/goal-setting, they are usually given wide latitude to pursue their more visionary causes and endeavors. Fail to "pay the rent" by doing the ministry basics, and nothing else that you propose will receive anything but grudging support. Paying the rent is a matter of trust-building, indeed covenant-making, that underlies and grounds all other ministry endeavors.

Unfortunately, in recent years this commonsensical wisdom has been labeled in some leadership circles as "mere chaplaincy." (Schaller himself, in my view, contributes to this confusion when he blithely says that paying the rent should never be a full-time job. He articulates a kind of scale of perfection that ranges from those who don't pay the rent at all, to those who only pay the rent, to those shining "transformational" leaders who seem to do it all.[24]) The leader who is occupied with such duties as regular visiting and riding the desk for long hours in sermon preparation may be spoken of condescendingly at the annual ministers' convocation as "old paradigm." Meanwhile the "new paradigms" of transformation and discipleship and the emerging church are hyped without regard to the need for grounding in the basic work of building relationships and trust.[25] Failure to invest in basic partnerships has doomed more than one transformational crusade. As Dietrich Bonhoeffer noted long ago, "Innumerable times a whole Christian community has broken down because it had sprung from a wish dream."[26]

Four, when the doings of ministry and leadership are a response to what they "suffer" or die to, and when leaders trust them as the "masks" of God at work in "what is immediately to hand," then anxiety does not so tightly grip the assembly. It would be odd indeed if a certain grace-given contentment, not to say complacency, did not accompany our work and doings. As Luther pastorally remarks, in our vocation "we are content to do what is immediately to hand and not to seek to master and control the future."[27]

The no-win situation of having responsibility within the household, he warns, is either arrogance on the one side or worry on the other. The leader "must watch out that his heart does not come to rely on these deeds of his, and get arrogant when things go well or worried when things go wrong. Just take the arrogance and worry out of watchfulness, and let it proceed in faith."[28]

So great is Luther's concern with this catch-22 of ministry that he makes the astonishing recommendation that those in authority "should proceed as if there were no God and they had to rescue themselves and manage their own affairs; just as the head of a household is supposed to work as if he were trying to sustain himself by his own labors."[29] Superficially, this advice doesn't sound very "religious." Actually, it's the consequence of what Luther says elsewhere about letting God be God by dying to the habitual and neurotic temptation to "play God." Such advice is like warning Adam and Eve that they have plenty to do in the rest of the garden without also trying to shinny up the tree of the knowledge of good and evil (Gen. 2:15–17). The cross calls us to be reconciled to our creaturely limits and to embrace our human condition.

In the last twenty years or so, much has been rightly made about the importance of the leader's "non-anxious presence." This concept comes from family systems theory as pioneered clinically by Murray Bowen and Edwin Friedman.[30] The theory has it that a leader or the head of a household who is self-composed stands in the midst of an anxiety-wrought group, with its emotional chaos, and by dint of her or his unruffled presence and demeanor enables the group to calm down enough to begin to think more clearly about itself and its doings.

But in what is this "calm-amid-the storm" presence and self-composure *theologically* rooted and grounded? Clearly, it is not a human possibility, for to be human is to be anxious. Humanly, one might "take the edge off" by therapeutic treatment or stoic resolve and discipline. But real transformation can happen only under the sway of the cross—that is, for those who come to confess that "I have been crucified with Christ; and it is no longer I who live, but it is Christ who lives in me. And the life I now live in the flesh I live by faith in the Son of God, who loved me and gave himself for me" (Gal. 2:19–21).

Only dying to self takes the worry, and its evil twin, arrogance, out of our watchfulness and enables us to proceed in faith, active in the works of love. Cross-shaped leadership and ministry are a response to the angelic Christmas and Easter proclamation, "Be not afraid."

In my faith tradition, we say that it takes three things to make something a sacrament: (1) it's commanded by Christ ("do this"); (2) it makes use of an earthly element (water, bread, wine) as its medium; and (3) it has some promise of grace attached to it. This is why we recognize only baptism and the Lord's Supper as God-ordained "means of grace" or sacraments.

What I have always believed is that ministry is in this respect a *virtual* sacrament. Though not physical in nature, the "doings of the saints" are like the earthly "elements" that God may adopt as "masks" of God's work in disguise. The makeup of these earthly masks is quite ordinary. The most commonplace encounters and situations of daily life (our loves, our laughters, our failures, our plans and ambitions, our sacrifices) in the world are the material elements of its servant action.

True Crosses and False Crosses

Just as there is a difference between Jesus's suffering and our suffering, we must recognize another distinction in the life of faith and ministry. In this earthly life and in ministry, there are true crosses and false crosses. On earth not every cross should be suffered and endured. Many earthly crosses are false crosses thrust upon us by an abusive world, random circumstances, or our own stupidity and sinfulness.

There is no official list of true and false crosses of the earthly variety. Jesus gives us only a general rule of thumb for cross-bearing: when it's "for the sake of the gospel" (Mark 8:35), it just might be a true cross to bear in faith. (Always remember, though: even true cross-bearing, which may help spread the gospel or serve the neighbor or mortify the flesh, does not atone for anything.) The trouble is that we don't always know when this is the case, do we? Only years of participating in a community of support, with its worship and prayer and spiritual direction and servant life, lead to such discernment. There are no quick fixes for the dilemma of distinguishing true from false earthly crosses. In ministry, as in life, we learn as we go. Yet the discernment is far from haphazard.

Nevertheless, let me offer the following three images as a stimulus to our mutual discernment. Picture these scenes:

First, in the 2005 movie *Kingdom of Heaven*, which tells the story of the time between the Second and Third Crusades, the Crusader Kingdom of Jerusalem sends an army out to face in battle the great Muslim leader Saladin. At the head of the Christian army is a giant, gold-encrusted and adorned cross, containing what is supposedly a fragment of the "true cross" from Jesus's crucifixion. One thinks of the Hebrew armies carrying the Ark before them in battle (Josh. 6).

When the battle of Hattin, as it is called historically, turns out to be a trap, and the crusaders are virtually annihilated, we see the wreckage of the golden processional cross/battle standard lying in ruins amid the dead and dying on the battlefield. We look upon the ruins of a lost cause and behold its false cross of human devising and pomposity.

Second, the award-winning 1986 film *The Mission* opens with the spectacle of an unnamed Jesuit priest being martyred by native people of South America in the eighteenth century. The priest has been lashed to a makeshift cross and placed in the river rapids at the head of a waterfall where, after shooting the rapids, he plunges over the falls to his death. Later, a repentant mercenary and adventurer in the same locale undergoes the prescribed penance of climbing the cliffs beside these same falls with a huge satchel of armor and weapons representing the baggage of his former life. At a certain height, the native people, with the agreement of the religious order, consent to his throwing the weapons over the falls. We view the overall process of penance as backbreaking and even masochistic. (Perhaps it's no accident that the opening scene of martyrdom depicts someone "going down," while the later scene of penance depicts someone "climbing up." It's like a metaphor of death and resurrection.) But oh, what a theatrical spectacle! It's compelling in all its historical authenticity and graphic detail.

Uneasily, though, we find ourselves asking: is such physical brutality and self-mortification a true or false cross? Frankly, I find myself torn, because on the one hand the penitential process suffers from the appearance of good works, but on the other hand what the repentant mercenary undergoes, what he "suffers," serves as a powerful and authentic witness that wins the trust of the native people whom he then goes on sacrificially to aid.

Third, at the 2006 National Youth Gathering of the Evangelical Lutheran Church in America, there was a daily venue called "Chat with a Bishop." These were one-hour sessions in which bishops from around the United States took turns answering questions in a town-meeting format. In the session I sat in on, most of the questions were what you would expect: inquiries about the church's social stances on such issues as abortion, world hunger, sexual orientation, and so forth.

But then one youth from Ohio spoke up and asked the bishop du jour, "Why are a lot of the crosses I see in churches so pretty? That doesn't make sense to me." At first this question took the bishop off guard. To his credit, he asked for clarification, and then opened up the floor for general discussion. The youth said, "I mean, shouldn't the cross be all gnarly and rough, not pretty?" Others in the group, both adults and youth, began to talk in very personal terms about what the cross meant to them. The whole history of how art has depicted the cross, and the theological subtleties of crucifixes versus empty crosses, etc., seemed quite beside the point. Here a young Christian, then others, engaged in the most basic struggle of the life of faith: the discernment of true and false earthly crosses. The one thing he knew was that "pretty" doesn't tell the gospel truth.

Author, educator, and activist Parker Palmer has spoken eloquently about the difference between true and false crosses in the spiritual life. He advocates *resistance* as the proper response to any cross that enters one's earthly life: "Resist any cross that comes your way. Boldly become a pole of opposition; live the contradiction. The false crosses will fall away, while those we must accept will stay there in the middle of our lives, pulling right and left, up and down, until they open us to our true center, a center where we are one with God, a center which we find only on the way of the cross."[31]

Resistance. This might seem an odd stance for those who confess that what they undergo or "suffer" is central to their vocation. But no. Resistance in this case is a response to earthly suffering, not to Christ's heavenly suffering, by which the world is made righteous. We resist earthly suffering with all our might precisely because the suffering saves nobody.

Moreover, we cannot know from appearances if such earthly cross-bearing, whether ours or others', serves to spread the gospel, help the neighbor, or tame our self-centered nature. It may not ennoble a thing; it may, and often does, merely victimize. Only when we have resisted to the last breath dare we judge whether any cross-bearing has been a ministry and therefore a true cross that remains in the center of our lives. Even then, we walk by faith, not by sight.

Many years ago I worked in a two-point parish, a pair of rural congregations served by one pastor. Additionally, each of these congregations was part of what's called a "union church." A union church was a phenomenon of early America in which two Protestant denominations, Lutheran and Reformed, coexisted in the same building and shared ministries while retaining their separate denominational identities. So, in this case the two-point parish consisted of four congregations, two Lutheran and two Reformed, with one pastor from each denomination running a ministry relay. Trust me: serving a union church is a lot like the famous Abbott and Costello baseball sketch, "Who's on first?"

Both "points" of the parish were trying to decide whether and how to break their union and to reorganize. Effectiveness of mission was at stake. Would a given union consolidate and form one congregation aligned with one denomination? Or would one member of the union buy out the other, and then the two groups go their separate ways? Or would they do nothing at all? The team guiding the two parishes consisted of the two on-site pastors, a lawyer, and a bishop and a conference minister with their respective assistants.

During the two-year study process, the two union congregations behaved in opposite ways. One debated vigorously and openly, sometimes angrily and not without a certain amount of rancor. Finger-pointing and raised voices were common currency. The other was outwardly polite and seemingly untroubled by the potential change and what each group might have to sacrifice. All went smoothly and uneventfully, and we on the advisory team felt that the latter union, with its lack of open hostility and public bickering, was going to reach consensus without incident.

Of course we were dead wrong. The "fightin' cousins" reached consensus while the "make nice" folks, in passive-aggressive fashion, dug in and refused to make any decision at all. The members of the outwardly battling and resistant group were actually coming to terms with, and taking ownership of, their new life. *They were active participants in dying in order to be reborn.* They have since moved on and have a thriving congregation with a strong sense of mission. We (preachers, lawyers, and bishops) learned to our dismay and professional embarrassment that the calm surface of the other congregation was a façade and really signaled the opposite: no one was coming to terms with anything, least of all the birth pangs of a new community life. Resist, then, with all your might any earthly cross that comes your way. It is one human means that God has given us to sort out true from false cross-bearing. True and false crosses are typically disguised. Classically, theology of the cross says we know God under the sign of opposites; the cross directs us to find God in the *least* likely places, often amid turmoil and contradiction. And because of this mystery, it is only in a community of support, in a living assembly of believers under the Word, in *mutual* ministry, that we can distinguish true from false cross-bearing. Martin Luther calls such discernment the "mutual consolation and conversation of brothers and sisters."[32]

The Basics of Cross-Shaped Leadership

As a young pastor, I often heard my dad tell me that people expected their ministers to be "cut from finer cloth," but also to be down-to-earth and "one of the guys." "Dad," I said, "that's impossible." "Right," he said. "Get used to it." He was onto something: the basics of cross-shaped leadership.

The Cross: Theology of the cross means that we know God in the midst of suffering, contradiction, turmoil, and the world's resistance to God's grace. It is the knowledge of faith as firsthand experience rather than as religious theory. The cross is God happening to us in real time and space. It is the call for us to be reconciled to the fullness of our human existence and to trust that in Jesus, through the power of the Spirit, God has done all the saving there is to be done. Taking up the cross is dying and rising with Christ; it is the doing of God to us; it is the death of our god-illusion.

The Cross and Vocation: Under the cross, we fulfill our calling not only in what we do, but in what we undergo or "suffer." Whether in daily life or its public offices, ministry's functioning is subject to death and resurrection; it dies to itself and rises anew even as it is undertaken. Christian vocation, including public leadership, is action in passion. Practically, *leadership as action in passion* means that its ministries are always provisional, contextual, and fallible. They are interim in character.

Two Kinds of Suffering: Jesus's passion and our passion are alike yet radically different. Jesus's suffering is of heaven, and bears the weight of atoning for the world's sins; it works righteousness before God. Our suffering is earthly and may help spread the gospel, serve the neighbor, or discipline us in our human nature.

Ministry as God's "Masks": Because the cross redirects our gaze and our ministry efforts back where they belong—that is, into the realm of the earthly and bodily needs of our neighbor—the ordinary and commonplace routines and settings of everyday life become the "masks" veiling God at work in God's presence and call.

True and False Crosses: Among the earthly crosses we are called to take up and bear, some are true and some are false. Not all earthly crosses spread the gospel, serve the neighbor, or tame our human egocentricity. Many earthly crosses only abuse and victimize us and others. Until a true earthly cross reveals itself, the Christian life, and its ministry, remains vigilant and practices active resistance to all earthly passion and suffering.

◈ Questions for Discussion and Reflection

1. Read Mark's account of the passion either in its long (Mark 14:1–15:47) or short (Mark 15:1–39 [40–47]) form. Instead of asking yourself or the group, "What does it mean?" ask

instead, "What is it *doing* to me? Does it comfort and console? Does it make me feel guilty? Does it leave me in awe or confusion? What makes it the passion? Who is undergoing what at whose hands?"

2. How do the official, public vision and mission statements of your ministry setting differ from the unconscious reasons for which the group seems really to have come together?

3. Mentors often say, "Pick your battles." Not every issue should be turned into the last stand at Thermopylae, the Alamo, or Bunker Hill. Think of a parish battle that you regret having fought. Think of one that you wish you *had* fought. How do you discern when to take a stand and when not to?

4. Do you find yourself wondering if you are "at the end of a chapter" or "at the end of the book" in your present ministry? Other than "testing the waters" by going for various interviews, what else could you be doing by way of collegial and professional discernment and spiritual direction? When, if ever, is it appropriate to speak and pray with a trusted and mature congregational member about the matter?

OLD SELF, NEW SELF
Beyond the Glittering Image

Every one of us is shadowed by an illusory person: a false self. This is the man I want myself to be but who cannot exist, because God does not know anything about him. And to be unknown of God is altogether too much privacy. —Thomas Merton[1]

This false self must die if we are to live, but since it is the only self we know we struggle to keep it alive and often lose it only when we are overwhelmed by the cross. —Parker Palmer[2]

To be raised up into the new creation, we don't need to be good, holy, smart, accountable, or even faithful: we only need to be dead.
—Robert Farrar Capon[3]

We must stand on the ground when the Savior comes and not float up into the air. —Christoph Blumhardt[4]

Not long ago a distant relative sent me some memorabilia of my grandfather. The Rev. Edward Berntsen was a Lutheran pastor who served in Wisconsin, North Dakota, and Minnesota. He worked as a hospital chaplain at the end of his career. He died long before I was born.

A formal portrait of my grandfather, whose image I had never seen, reveals a long, narrow face with equine nose and searching eyes. He has a faraway look. With his full mustache and swept-back hair, he looks like the movie actor Jeff Daniels playing a historical role. Those who knew him say that he was a quiet man, perhaps a bit distant, and not the best public speaker.

Looking at his picture sitting on my office credenza, I wonder whether my grandfather and I are at all alike in temperament. In this life, I'll never know. However, two snapshots of me during adolescence could well bookend my grandfather's portrait. They tell the tale of an emerging self.

One black-and-white snapshot shows a junior-high youth coming up the sidewalk of his home after school. He has slung over his shoulder a pair of sweatpants whose drawstrings are tied to make a bag in which he carries his sweaty clothes from basketball practice. The look on his face is decidedly empty and emotionless, "flat of affect," as the psychologists like to put it. In his eyes, you can see his grandfather's faraway look.

Fast-forward a couple of years. A color snapshot is a real "Kodak moment." The student is standing in his bedroom next to a bulletin board covered with ribbons, awards, news articles, and certificates of various kinds, including report cards that display his achievements. He is fit and trim, the result of miles of running. But again, his face is vacant, as if all of the documented proof notwithstanding, there is grave doubt about who this emerging young adult is.

Four years pass. He's on a train heading for Boston and the Massachusetts Mental Health Center to undertake those probing standardized psychological tests that are a prelude to the examination process for ministry in the church.

There were two such lonely train rides, the second to have the clinical psychologist interpret his test results. As with many young ministerial candidates, this was his first experience of having his fragile psyche poked and prodded by a stranger. It was an Orwellian ("Big Brother") experience.

When the psychologist asked him what kinds of things really tended to upset him, he said that it might be little things like the nicks and scratches on his new leather briefcase, which he held clutched in his hands on his lap. The big picture, he added, didn't faze him. No doubt the doctor feasted on this obsession. (Later in life, the young man would become pretty adept at hanging wallpaper.)

What did take him aback was the doctor's prediction that in the years ahead, the young man would always find himself torn between the love of parish ministry and a passion for books, scholarship, and the arts. The doctor said that this was just who the candidate was and that he should learn to live creatively with the tension. There was no use trying to force himself into one mold or the other, the psychologist said. To do so would be artificial and cause much unnecessary grief.

Of course, the young man didn't listen to the doctor. As he took the train home down the I-95 corridor, he vowed to beat the system. He would resolve the tension in his soul by sheer force of will, working to become either a brilliant scholar or the greatest "churchman" since the early apostles. No sense being who you are when you might triumph by dividing your soul and putting your supposedly best foot (self) forward, right?

Alas, the good doctor was spot-on. In the years to come the young man would pour all his energies and passion into trying to suppress or exalt one part of his self or the other. The shadow game couldn't go on forever. Some significant life failures and a couple of health crises gave the lie to the whole grandiose enterprise of reinventing himself. Before it was too late, it was time to begin the recovery of what Parker Palmer has called "the hidden wholeness."[5]

Baptism and Temptation: Retracing the Steps of Adam and Eve

The recovery of our "hidden wholeness," and what this means for our formation as leaders, is a journey on the way to the cross from the waters of baptism through the wilderness of temptation. It's a journey that retraces the footsteps of our first parents, Adam and Eve. According to St. Paul's letters, we are born of the Old Adam, but in Christ crucified and risen, we are reborn of the New Adam (1 Cor. 15:22). The Old Adam, one might say, is the Adam and Eve of fig-leaf fame hiding out in the Garden of Eden with God stalking them. The New Adam, Christ, comes forth from the garden tomb of Easter and remakes the children of Adam and Eve to be a new creation. Baptism is entrance into this new creation. Named and reclaimed by God, a person receives a new identity, and with it a new vocation.

Have you noticed that in Matthew, Mark, and Luke, Jesus's

baptism and his temptation in the wilderness come one after the other? Something's going on here, and this something has to do in part with Jesus's finding and testing his identity and vocation. Much of the gospel finds people pressuring and tempting Jesus to abandon his true identity as the suffering Messiah and trusting child of God.

The critical moment in Jesus's baptism comes when God's voice declares that Jesus is the Father's "beloved, with whom I am well-pleased." In Matthew it's a public declaration: "This is my Son" (Matt. 3:17). In Mark and Luke it's spoken directly to Jesus: "You are my Son" (Mark 1:11; Luke 3:22). Either way, what defines Jesus is his belovedness. He is assured that he is God's child. On this he will depend all the way to the cross. On the strength of this promise he will draw for endurance in his mission, especially when the world and those around him reject or misunderstand him and try to divert him from this mission. In baptism, and later at the Transfiguration, Jesus takes hold of the belovedness at the core of his being. This is his empowerment, an empowerment *received, not achieved*. This is his true self. So, too, asserts Thomas Merton's protégé James Finely: "Our true self is a received self."[6]

When Jesus is led into the wilderness by the Spirit to be tempted by the devil, his identity, his true self, is tested. *Are you really God's beloved child? Do you think this God of yours will actually take care of you?* Such are the seeds of doubt the devil tries to sow in Jesus's heart and mind. Whether the temptation is to turn stones into bread (Matt. 4:3) or to force God's hand by jumping off the Temple to prove that God will rescue him (Matt. 4:6) or to trade his soul for power and glory over the world (Matt. 4:9), the anatomy of temptation is exposed. If you can convince someone that he or she is unloved or uncared for, then you can pretty much sell him or her anything to make up for the feared deprivation. Just drop some heavy hints that God might not be all that trustworthy or that the goodness of life is questionable at best, and you tempt a person to construct his own god-project to compensate for the neglect and abandonment he believes he has suffered.

Since these injuries are a very real part of our lives, the devil's got some pretty sharp tools with which to work. No wonder the next bottle of Jack Daniels, the next lottery ticket, the next award or accomplishment, the next love, the next pleasure or possession, the next campaign of revenge seems to promise the easing of our pain and recompense for our supposed wounding at life's hands.

It has been said that the essence of temptation is wanting to be like God *without* God.[7] The Jewish and Christian Scriptures insist that humans are made in the image of God. For Christians, perhaps it's more accurate to say that humans "image the image," since Jesus himself is the "image of the invisible God" (Col. 1:15). Our life is "hidden with Christ in God" (Col. 3:3). This declaration means that our true self is our self hidden with God; our false self is our self apart from God. The false self is a prisoner of mistrust and wants to live in its own strength—to be like God without God. The false self doesn't understand the famous pronouncement of W. R. Inge: "Christianity promises to make men free; it never promises to make them independent."[8]

From St. Augustine through Martin Luther and John Calvin, to such a modern spiritual figure as Thomas Merton, runs a common thread of theological interpretation about the human self. This interpretation is but a recap of what the Bible, in particular St. Paul, says about human identity from Adam and Eve to Christ. Humankind is born in Adam but reborn in Christ's dying and rising. At creation God graces us with a self that is whole. The self is the inmost core of our human being. It's our "who-ness," as I like ungrammatically to put it. And in this world we are all residents of "Whoville" (with apologies to Dr. Seuss's irascible Grinch who stole Christmas)!

But the gift of the self—and it is a gift—becomes deformed. It loses its wholeness. The tragedy of this deformation is the drama of temptation and the fall into sin. Humankind wants to go its own way and to live in its own strength, so the self becomes, as Augustine and Luther put it, "curved in upon itself." Rather than live in covenant with God and the neighbor, the self turns inward and feeds on itself. So it becomes a false self, the opposite of what its creator wills. The Grinch-self holed up in his mountain cave, indeed!

Martin Luther aptly describes the false self as the "old Adam" or the "old creature" (*alter Mensch*). In his commentary on Romans, he puts it this way: "The term 'old man' describes what kind of person is born of Adam, not according to his nature but according to the defect of his nature. For his nature is good, but the defect is evil."[9] This is orthodox teaching. Evil is not something in itself; it's not some independent principle or "substance." Rather, *evil is always good gone bad*. Even at its worst, evil is never outside the reach of God. In the midst of evil, God is still God.

For Luther, after Paul in Romans 6, baptism enacts the self's death and resurrection. Its "power and effect," as he insists, is nothing less than

> the slaying of the old Adam and the resurrection of the new creature, both of which must continue our whole life long. Thus a Christian life is nothing else than a daily baptism, begun once and continuing ever after. For we must keep at it without ceasing, always purging whatever pertains to the old Adam, so that whatever belongs to the new creature may come forth.[10]

For Luther, our true self is both a gift and a task. Not half and half, but completely one and completely the other! We live with the tension.

Like a wise counselor, Luther takes an inventory of the old creature's way of functioning: "irascible, spiteful, envious, unchaste, greedy, lazy, proud—yes—and unbelieving."[11] Yet because baptism remains forever, we always have access to its grace and therefore to the strength to "suppress" and to "subdue" the old creature in us.[12] So baptism empowers people to do what they cannot do on their own, which is "to keep at it without ceasing." In baptism, dying and rising with Christ is here and now. The "I" that wants to live apart from God and neighbor, says Luther in his commentary on Galatians, is crucified with Christ and subdued by the cross.[13] The true self is a cross-shaped self, a self reconciled to its full humanity.

Where Luther is a pastor, preacher, and Bible commentator, John Calvin, from the second generation of the Protestant Reformation, organizes Christian teaching into what has the surface appearance of a system of doctrine, but which is really contemplative in its intent and force.[14] His theological masterpiece, *Institutes of the Christian Religion,* defines the knowledge of God as intimately connected with the knowledge of the human self. He begins, "Without knowledge of self there is no knowledge of God."[15]

Because the two—that is, the knowledge of God and that of self—are so closely connected, Calvin muses, "which precedes and brings forth the other is not easy to discern."[16] Although what the Geneva Reformer calls the "order of right teaching" requires that we always begin our theologizing with the knowledge of God, it's nevertheless true that "the knowledge of ourselves not only arouses us to seek God, but also, as it were, leads us by the hand to find him."[17] And yet, this knowing of God remains reflexive: "Again, it is certain that man never achieves a clear knowledge of himself unless he has first looked upon God's face, and then descends from contemplating him to scrutinize himself."[18] In the order of revelation, knowing God precedes knowing ourselves not in a contemplative ascent, but rather a descent.

The True Self and the False Self

The Trappist Thomas Merton is a modern heir of this whole tradition. Merton's profound approach to the Christian life and spiritual practice centers on the war waged within the human soul between the true self and the false self. Merton views prayer and contemplation as the path of the true self's rediscovery.

For Merton, sin is *the* monumental case of mistaken identity. Sin is, as we might say these days, a case of "identity theft." For Christian tradition to say that humans are born in sin, explains Merton, is to say that we are congenitally shadowed by a false self. "I was born in a mask. I came into existence under a sign of contradiction, being someone that I was never intended to be and therefore a denial of what I am supposed to be."[19] The false self is chronically a "private self," one that wants to exist in its own strength, apart from God's will and God's love. "And such a self cannot help but be an illusion."[20]

The false self is all wrapped up in egocentric desires. Everything in the universe must revolve around this "I," this "self." Life itself is used up "in the desire for pleasures and the search for experiences, for power, honor, knowledge and love, to clothe this false self and construct its nothingness into something objectively real."[21] Merton's description of the false self is poignant, even heartrending. It reminds you of a B movie about an invisible man, a man who is unreal but does not know it: "And I wind experiences around myself and cover myself with pleasures and glory like bandages in order to make myself perceptible to myself, and to the world, as if I were an invisible body that could only become visible when something visible covered its surface."[22]

For Merton, no human being can find his or her true self. The true self remains hidden in God's keeping. So, what's an invisible man or woman to do? He declares, as does the tradition before him, that the mission begins at baptism. The only one who can teach us to find God, he insists, is God alone. If I find this God, "I will find myself and if I find my true self I will find Him." The life of faith, the Christian life, is nothing else than to "pray for your own discovery." In the life of prayer and contemplative practice, which for Merton is in no way a human work, "God utters me like a word containing a partial thought of Himself."[23]

Merton's invisible man, who "winds experiences around himself" to make himself real to himself, is a stepchild of Luther's (and Augustine's) "irascible, spiteful, envious, unchaste, greedy, lazy, proud—yes—and unbelieving" old creature who is curved in upon himself. To be "lost," Merton says, is "to be left to . . . the smoke-self that must inevitably vanish." To be "saved," on the other hand, is "to return to one's inviolate and eternal reality and to live in God."[24] The mystical, contemplative Merton then concludes: "We become contemplatives when God discovers Himself in us."[25] The contemplative life, rooted in baptism, is a God-given means for dismantling the false self and recovering the true self in union with a loving God.

Merton's description of the true self and the false self comes about as close to an orthodox spiritual theology of human personality as one is likely to get in Christian faith traditions. To probe further into this theme of the self's quest for rediscovery and rebirth, one must turn to the pioneering secular work of a figure like

Karen Horney, a so-called neo-Freudian analyst of the first half of the twentieth century, whose delineation of the idealized self in neurosis and human growth is remarkably true to our everyday experience with one another. Where Merton speaks of the true self, Horney speaks of the "real self," while Merton's false self is much like Horney's "idealized self."

Working with her patients, Horney observed that human growth is a process of self-realization. In growing up, a person will, given the chance, develop his or her own specific human potentialities. A "real self" emerges that constitutes "that central inner force common to all human beings and yet unique in each, which is the deep source of growth."[26]

What makes up this central inner force or core? Horney speaks of "potentialities" and sometimes more informally of the thoughts, wishes, interests, gifts, willpower, clarity, and depth of one's feelings. Though this raw material of the soul is common to all people, its combination in a given person is specific and unique. It's like the DNA of the soul, one might say. The purpose and task of growth at the core of the human person is the formation of an intact, whole, and unique self. Unhindered, the real self will grow toward such self-realization. It will form a healthy identity and carry out its mission in the world.[27]

Of course, the key word is "unhindered." Growing up is rarely if ever unhindered; as with the weather, favorable conditions don't always prevail. Parents and caregivers may be overprotective, overindulgent, erratic, indifferent, distant, picky, judgmental, hypocritical, irritable, or cold. So the growth of the real self is inevitably skewed and becomes "split" and distorted.[28] The self forfeits its birthright wholeness.

Horney detected in her patients three different unconscious life strategies for coping with the real self's experience of deprivation: *the self moves toward, against, or away from others.*[29] In layperson's terms, we become either overagreeable, clinging, and people-pleasing (toward); or hostile, aggressive, and "in your face" (against); or aloof and above it all (away). We form an "idealized self" in which one of these three modes of daily functioning predominates. The others recede into the shadows of the soul. The self, now idealized (out of whack!), imagines it has found a solution for the hurts and slights of its environment. In truth, it has only forfeited its wholeness.

By adopting one of the three unconscious life strategies in relating to others, the self undergoes a "one-sided development." This "solution" to its predicament carries a price. Large areas of the individual's personality become unavailable for constructive uses. And thus he or she now "desperately needs self-confidence, or a substitute for it." This skewed development results in an urgent need "to lift himself above others." Horney calls this effort "the search for glory." In this process, really a silent epic quest, the person "endows himself with unlimited powers and with exalted faculties; he becomes a hero, a genius, a supreme lover, a saint, a god."[30]

Self-idealization becomes self-glorification, and each person builds up his or her unique self-image to fill his or her unmet needs. "Compliance becomes goodness; love, saintliness; aggressiveness becomes strength, leadership, heroism, omnipotence; aloofness becomes wisdom, self-sufficiency, independence."[31] What seems to be a "solution" becomes a neurosis, or as we call it in slang terms, a "hang-up." It becomes a person's modus operandi for everyday living. The aim of treatment is to help restore some semblance of wholeness to the self.

To read Horney's laundry list of our personal hang-ups makes you want to go hunting for a fig leaf.

The Self in Ministry Practice

The thesis of this chapter is that readiness for public leadership in the church is tied to the cruciform rebirth of the true self. To some degree, all of us are shadowed by a false or illusory person, an imposter, who accompanies us into the public arena. For all of us, there is at least some split in our souls between our true self and our false self. The imposter or false self is the self we put forward as our whole self, when in fact it is a distortion of our whole, and thus true, self.

The one-sided development of the self is expressed in one of several "shoulds." Horney calls them "inner mandates."[32] My own take on her description of inner mandates is this: there is the leader who believes, "I *should* be compassionate, caring, nice, self-sacrificing, holy." And there is the leader who believes, "I *should* be decisive, prophetic, authoritative, acclaimed." And there is the leader who believes, "I *should* be set apart, faultless, self-sufficient, expert, wise." The false self attempts to lift itself (i.e., the "search for glory") above its woundedness, its one-sided development, by resorting to these exaggerated inner "shoulds."

Let's informally illustrate these tendencies with portraits of leaders, or those in training, whom we may have known. The self's search for glory, its god-project, wears many faces.

Helen is a sixty-two-year-old woman who loves volunteer work at her church. She is active in the women's groups and in Sunday school. She is quiet, kind, and compassionate, and cares deeply about the sick and others who need healing and support. She is prayerful. Though not paid, she has attained the unofficial status of a deaconess-like staff member. Her work is appreciated, and she receives frequent praise from the regular worshipers for her self-sacrificing ways.

Helen's husband left her many years ago. For good and for ill, the congregation is her "family." She has been told that she ought to consider becoming a pastor. It seems to be the next logical step in her calling. Besides, the church has been a safe place for her where she is able to avoid conflict with people. She doesn't seem to understand, though, that in her faith tradition there are many callings, and that none of them has any more dignity than another; there is no scale of merit or rank in Christian vocation. Though it has been years since she was in a classroom, she would like to go to seminary. When her candidacy committee asks her how she plans to afford it, she says that she will cash in her pension to pay the tuition.

Then she is asked a crucial question: "What can you do as a pastor—that is, as public representative of the church—that you aren't already doing in your much-appreciated ministry as a baptized Christian? Why do you want to become an ordained minister?" With great hesitation and not a little sadness in her voice, she responds, "I thought maybe you could tell me."

At this moment, her interviewers know that it would be wrong for Helen to go forward with the process. Her sense of call to ordained ministry lacks clarity. Moreover, all Christians are called to be "helpful and kind." This call says little about leadership or public ministry in the church. She is already exercising her God-given gifts in important ministry as a baptized Christian. Her exaggerated need to be needed bespeaks a false self that wants to cling too closely to other people to be of real—that is, selfless—service to them.

Colin has had what can only be described as a "stormy" career in the church. Gifted, passionate, and at times confrontational, he sees himself as a prophetic voice for social justice and for those who are marginalized by society and even the church. Before he resigned from the clergy roster altogether, he worked in a variety of settings as an ordained minister.

While Colin delights in challenging authority—"sticking it to the man," as he puts it—his work history has been erratic. He has not been reliable in carrying out the ordinary tasks and duties of his various ministry assignments. Sometimes he has been caught in lies. However, given his family background, the only world he knows is that of a pastor, so he has applied for reinstatement to the ministerial office. Even his dress reflects his stance of defiance, however. When he comes to the formal interview for his reinstatement, he dresses down as a matter of principle. When he is asked whether this is his way of sending a message to those in power, he says, "Yeah." When the committee follows up by asking how he would feel if personal appearance became an obstacle to serving the very people he claims to champion, he falls silent. Yet his personal hostility is never far from the surface. Colin's false self finds enemies on every front; his aggressive, even attacking, personal style always moves against the world. His readiness to serve is severely impaired. His reinstatement is denied.

Sarah is a "pipeliner," a young person who has come to the seminary straight out of college. She is bright, sunny in disposition, creative, and fun to be around. Multitalented, Sarah has a mature faith and, considering her age, a strong and clear sense of call to ordained ministry. She is compassionate and well spoken. She is admired by her peers and looked to for leadership in student government at the seminary. Sarah is a genuine "star" on the rise.

As a child, Sarah was sexually molested by an extended-family member. She goes to counseling on a regular basis to work at her issues. She can be prone to depression. One of her tendencies is to avoid conflict and potentially confrontational situations. What this trait will mean in the normal rough and tumble of parish practice is of concern to her mentors. Faced with an angry or obstinate parishioner or a contentious committee meeting, she might withdraw and shrink from all interaction. Being appropriately assertive in leadership situations could be a very real problem.

But Sarah has "the right stuff," not just in terms of talent and her sense of call, but also in her personal resilience. She seems able to do what Martin Luther urged those who face personal trials: "to keep at it without ceasing." She follows the recommendations of her mentors and focuses even more on her counseling work, plus working in a variety of ministry settings to broaden her practical experience. Eventually, Sarah's readiness is apparent, and she enters the ranks of clergy as an effective and dedicated pastor. When she is overstressed or "running on empty," Sarah will need to remain vigilant about her false self's tendency to flee in sudden movement away from the world. But in overcoming her wounded history, she has recovered the hidden wholeness of an intact and, so, true self.

Fifteen years ago—and in one week—I received confusing signals about my own person and work. At the beginning of the week I received a "poison-pen letter" from an angry parishioner. The elderly man accused me of not paying enough attention to his wife in the final stages of her battle with cancer. He also directed his ire at his relatives for their supposed neglect. He wrote that I was "a disgrace" and that the church "should be ashamed" that it had ever "hatched" me as a pastor. I was, he said, "the worst excuse for a pastor that I have ever known." That was not a good day.

The next Sunday a middle-aged man walked up to me after church and told me that I had "saved our church." "Only you could have done it, pastor," he effused. I went straight home and said to my wife, "I'm confused, honey. Am I a bum or a hero?" She said, "Yes." Ever since that week, I have come to believe that we are not who the world says we are. We're not even who *we* say we are. We are who God says we are at baptism.

When I evaluate my own "one-sided development," I realize that I fall firmly into the camp of those who deal with their issues by moving "away from others." Retreat into self-sufficiency and aloofness is my tendency when exhausted or under stress. In tribute to Muhammad Ali, I think of this tendency to retreat as emotional "rope-a-dope." Once I asked to see a neighboring pastor and to speak with him about some of my personal concerns. Though I was not on intimate terms with him, he was someone whom I respected. When I sat down in his office, the first thing he said to me was this: "Thanks for coming, John. But to tell you the truth, I'm surprised you're here. You've always come across to me, and to others, as cool, aloof, and self-sufficient—as if you had it all together." Though typed as introverted on most personality tests, I have usually been in the moderate range. My false self steps forward when I retreat from the world in full flight.

The "search for glory"—that is, the attempt to lift ourselves above our woundedness instead of coming to terms with it by entering into it—wears many faces, then: self-sufficiency and perfection, withdrawal, prophetic rage, or saintliness and neediness. Yet when restored to their "hidden wholeness," these exaggerations of our self can become true spiritual gifts. The movement toward others may be transformed into gifts of healing, mercy, compassion, encouragement, and helping. The movement against may be reshaped into gifts of advocacy, prophecy, leadership, teaching, or administration. The movement away from others may become the gifts of faith, discernment, patience, prayer, and active listening. (Please don't place these on a formal chart or grid! My understanding of such things is much more informal and fluid. I'm thinking in terms of loose clusters that gather around the vectors of the true self's movements.)

Baptism is the beginning of the end for the imposter or false self. The false self's program for substitute happiness is dismantled by the cross, by the drowning of the "old creature" and the rising of the "new creature." Yet in this life we must, again as Luther insists, "keep at it without ceasing." Short of eternal life, our self remains in an interim state of existence. It may fluctuate between degrees of truth and falsity during our earthly sojourn, but we never "arrive" at some pure, angelic state of being. The self is always provisional and fallible in its growth and development. On the way to its promised wholeness, our selfhood "suffers"—that is, it undergoes the passion of its transformation.

The Search for Glory in the Churches

Thirty years ago I visited some distant relatives in Norway. One day we went up into the mountains north of Oslo. We stayed in their mountain cabin just below the tree line. In the evening we turned on the television and happened to catch a news story about the enthronement of a newly elected bishop. The liturgy was extravagant, formal, and solemn. Incense, chant, and ornate vestments filled the cathedral with sensory radiance.

Then, with English subtitles on the screen, the commentator said, "When the church has lost its power, it still has its glory." As a young intern pastor, I was rendered speechless. That not only individuals but entire communities may consume themselves in a search for glory is a sobering realization. But why should we be surprised? A group as well as an individual has a self. And since "The self seeks itself in all things, even in its piety,"[33] the practice of religion in community may also be consumed by the "glory story" instead of the "cross story."

Faith traditions as well as individuals evidence the pattern of moving toward, against, or away from society and even creation itself. Fundamentalist evangelicals tend toward an aggressive, triumphalist, even hostile mode of functioning toward the surrounding society. It's not uncommon to find churches whose names, and message, contain a generous sprinkling of the words "victory" and "victorious living." Separatist traditions stand aloof from the world and hope to remain untainted or unstained by its supposed impurity. At the extremes this aloofness becomes cultlike. Then there are those who wholeheartedly embrace the entrepreneurial spirit and the values of a marketplace culture. "To identify needs and to meet them" (as if people knew what they need!) is the marketing formula for such ministry practice.

America in particular has provided rich soil for groups captivated by various versions of the glory story. As a frontier nation, we have always displayed a restless spirit that yearns to push beyond any boundary or confine. Spiritually, this has meant two things: one, the birth of some "American original" faith communities—the Church of Jesus Christ of Latter-day Saints (Mormons); the Church of Christ, Scientist (Christian Scientists); the Seventh-day Adventist Church; the Watchtower Bible and Tract Society, or Jehovah's Witnesses; Pentecostalism—and two, the makeover of historical churches (the so-called mainline churches) when they came on shore in the New World. New Age groups have also found a welcome climate in North America.

Historians tell us that the watershed religious event of the American frontier was the great revival at Cane Ridge, Kentucky, in 1801. Cane Ridge is to our spiritual history what Woodstock is to our social history a century and a half later. As many as twenty-five thousand disgruntled Presbyterians, Methodists, and Baptists came to Cane Ridge on August 6 and met for one week. With roots in rural Scottish sacramental Holy Fairs, the revival was filled with ecstatic experiences for the backwoodsmen and their families. Caught up in spiritual rapture, including "jerking" and "barking," the participants found that their denominational differences and even personal boundaries melted away and were erased.[34]

The legacy of Cane Ridge is what Yale literary and cultural critic Harold Bloom calls "The American Religion." It is really a revival of the ancient Gnostic groups, who believed that to know God meant freedom from history, time, nature, community, and other selves. Only a self who is in reality an *uncreated* spark of the divine can have such rapturous knowledge. It is this uncreated self—one free of all earthly makeup, limitations, and grounding—that is the seat of true "religion."[35] One is reminded of the infamous patient whom Karen Horney quotes as saying, "If it were not for reality, I would be perfectly all right."[36]

The nitty-gritty of creation and human history, to say nothing about a manger, a cross, and a grave, is an embarrassment to the spiritualizing tendencies of these disembodied religious traditions. We find ourselves floating up in an ethereal world alien to that of the Hebrew and Christian Scriptures, which proclaim "the mighty acts of God" in creation, history, and community as the earthly elements of faith. To worship a first-century C.E. Jewish carpenter from Palestine as "God in human flesh" ought to be scandalous to the otherworldly aspirations of such groups. And we are very far from Martin Luther's insistence that as disciples, "We are meant to be human beings, not divine."[37]

Today the great religious attraction in America is for "the gospel of abundance" and "purpose-driven" ministry. Every airport book kiosk is stacked with titles proclaiming "the best you yet." Spiritual seekers, no more frontiersmen but often dwellers in suburbia, are assured that if they will give their lives to Jesus in a deliberate act of will, a certain level of prosperity, purpose, or well-being will naturally flow toward them. Never mind that in this self-help arrangement, God does not do all the saving there is to be done but awaits our "decision" to complete the formula of salvation. Conveniently, this joining our will with God's gives rise to a "blueprint for living" that troubled souls can turn to, like the instruction sheet for assembling a piece of Swedish furniture. Lists of the "marks of discipleship" multiply like rabbits and even spawn a kind of spiritual strategic plan, corporate flow chart and all. Behold: the triumph of the idealized church self in all its exaggerated, ethereal glory.

One of the most prominent of these communities has as its public symbol not the cross but a three-dimensional polished metal globe that is center stage on the platform of its cavernous auditorium. Pulpits are clear Plexiglas podiums, as if we are no longer, as the Bible says, "seeing in a mirror, dimly," but now "face to face." And just as Wal-Mart and other companies of its kind are called "big box" retailers, so the church is a "big box" retailer of spiritual abundance.

Whether as an individual or a community, the "old creature" is cunning and resilient. At any life stage, or during any era, it can morph into the next false self in which we misplace our trust. As the word of the cross, the gospel proclaims the death of the old creature and the restoration of creation to wholeness. Salvation no longer means an escape from this world or a denial of our humanity, but rather, as the early church put it, that "the glory of God is a human fully alive" (Irenaeus).[38] On this gracious promise depends our formation as cross-shaped leaders.

How might cross-shaped leaders think, feel, and function on the basis of this liberating news? Consider these implications. *One*, the more secure the leader is in her true self, the more resilient she will be in the face of failure. For the false self, nothing is more horrible than failure, even the normal failures that are part of the fabric of daily life. The more whole and intact the self is, however, the more failure is taken in stride. It's still quite real, and it's still no fun, but it is not surprising, nor is it a death sentence. For the cross-shaped self, the promise of forgiveness underlies all else, and so this promise is the safety net of the self's (true or false!) very existence. Failure is very much an "option." Indeed, it is an integral part of carrying out the self's mission. Thus, the true self takes reasonable chances; it is not completely "risk averse." It lives by promise, not by the tyranny of perfection.

Two, the cross-shaped true self is flexible in its functioning. Its plans and projects are not fixed. And they are not fixed because they are not pretending thereby to save the world. Thus, the impact of change is also not so traumatic. Because cross-shaped ministry is always provisional, the leader expects to revise and change on the fly. Envisioning, goal-setting, and planning all go on, but there is no pretense of their being "written in stone."

Three, cross-shaped leaders are able to discern what their mission is—and what it is *not*. What makes this discernment possible is a deeper degree of self-knowledge. That we are equipped and have the resources to take on a particular challenge doesn't mean that it is ours. The true self is accustomed to asking, "Yes, we could do this, but would it be *us*?" And there may well be other ventures about which it says, "This has our name written all over it, so how can we get ourselves up to speed to tackle it?"

Taking hold in faith of the true self is the key that unlocks the door of vocation—for both individuals and communities. Yet knowing the true self is not a human possibility. The self must "suffer" death and be buried and on the third day rise again on the way to a New Creation.

Summary

1. The question of readiness for public leadership in the assembly is a matter of the self's struggle for wholeness. To some degree, all of us are shadowed by a false self, an imposter, who accompanies us into the public arena. The recovery of our true self is the promise of our baptismal birthright. On the way from baptism through temptation, the false self is dismantled at the foot of the cross. The true self is the cross-shaped self.

2. In this sinful world the self is prone to an exaggerated development toward, against, or away from others. To compensate for its one-sided development, the self tries to lift itself above others in a vain "search for glory" driven by a series of inner mandates or "shoulds" that hold the self captive.

3. Not only individuals but also communities are consumed by "the search for glory" in triumphalism, sect-like withdrawal, or cultural accommodation and conformity.

4. When restored to their hidden wholeness by the cross, the falsifications of the self (individual or group) are remade into the gifts of servant leadership and servant life.

❖ Questions for Discussion and Reflection

1. Read the full accounts of Jesus's temptation in the wilderness (Matt. 4:1–11; Luke 4:1–13). As a leader, when are you tempted to mistrust God's care and protection of you? When the devil "pushes your buttons," what kinds of attacks are you most vulnerable to, given who you are? What's the worst thing someone can accuse you of? For good and ill, to what do you resort to ease your pain? When you are "running on empty"— that is, when you are tired and stressed out—what is your tendency? Clinging to others? Being overaggressive toward them?

Running and hiding, giving the world the "silent treatment"? What "shoulds" or "inner mandates" most gnaw at you? What false self steps forward?

2. Think of a ministry venture that has your "name written all over it," but for which you must become equipped. Think of a venture at which you could well succeed but that simply "isn't you."

3. When church members ask, "Why can't we be more like that church across town," what kind of discussion follows?

YOUR LAST PROUD DAY
On Being Made Humble

The only complete righteousness is humility. —Martin Luther[1]

*Humility consists in being precisely the person you actually
are before God, and since no two people are alike, if you
have the humility to be yourself you will not be like anyone else
in the whole universe.* —Thomas Merton[2]

It's hard to be humble when you believe in magic. —Rob Furey[3]

Don't be so humble—you're not that great. —Golda Meir[4]

"This is your last proud day," began the preacher at our seminary graduation. Who could have known then that this was
more than an attention-getting "hook" to draw the assembly into the day's sermon? He was an African American preacher
from Philadelphia, the Rev. William Kennedy, who used to travel
all the way to New Haven to teach courses in the tradition of black
preaching. (Alas, I've tried to find out what became of him, but
to date no one at the seminary and none of the Philadelphia-area
veteran clergy whom I've asked seem to know.)

The preacher's text was from 1 Peter: "Humble yourselves therefore under the mighty hand of God, so that he may exalt you in
due time" (1 Pet. 5:6). Was he aware that 1 Peter was one of Martin
Luther's favorite Bible texts, and especially the cross-reference
from Proverbs, "God opposes the proud, but gives grace to the
humble" (1 Pet. 5:5; Prov. 3:34)?

After he read the text, he sauntered to the pulpit with carefree steps,
as if it were a "hazy, hot, and humid" day in the life of the Kingdom itself. Then the preacher delivered his opening line with a large parental

smile: "This is your last proud day." The second sentence was equally astonishing to the fresh-faced seminarians in the front pews of the chapel, with their proud families assembled behind them. "Because if you aren't humble now, when you go out into the churches, they will *make you* humble." There were audible gasps from the crowd.

Surely the preacher's prophetic warning couldn't be a foretaste of all the graduates' triumphs to come in the one holy, catholic, and apostolic church. Surely the clergy-in-waiting were destined for great things, even glory, or so thought many in the assembly. Swept up in the moment, how could the multitude know that glory would turn out to mean what it meant for the Jesus of John's Gospel, the "glory" of being "lifted up" on a cross (John 3:14)? Above all, how *could* they have known that this was not bad news, but indeed very good news?

For as it would unfold in the years to come, death and resurrection would be not only the subject of preaching, the heart of liturgy, and the spirit of pastoral care, but also the unseen influence shaping the leader's daily professional functioning. The leader would *be humbled* by her very work: by not always having the answers, by lack of giftedness for important ministries, by the need to apologize for insensitive remarks, by failure to keep commitments, by cowardice, by laxity in prayer, by anger and resentment toward "problem" people, and by disillusionment with the once-held ideal of the church. Yet there would be no glorious martyrdom to be recorded in the chronicles of church history. James Barrie, the sentimental author of *Peter Pan,* said, "Life is one long lesson in humility." So, too, is the practice of ministry.

The Grace of Humility

Both early and late in his career as a reformer, Martin Luther would say that the only conceivable preparation for receiving God's grace is *humility.* There is some dispute among scholars as to what this stress on humility means. Stemming from the thought of St. Augustine, and as developed by the traditions of medieval spirituality, humility was a virtue those in monasteries and convents were expected to practice. Luther was no stranger to this emphasis.

However, given Luther's basic teaching on justification by grace through faith, humility is really synonymous with faith itself. The two are virtually interchangeable. For someone like Luther, humility is utterly real, yet not a natural human capacity. In no way is humility a human work. Humility is the face worn by those who have been made righteous by faith. Passively (see chapter 1), people are *made* humble. Humility is nothing other than being reduced to the state in which we claim absolutely nothing before God. It's at the core of that "undergoing," that action in passion, of which we spoke in chapter 1. As with faith, when we grope to speak of humility, we reach the limits of human language itself:

> First, God has assuredly promised his grace to the humble, that is, to those who lament and despair of themselves. But no man can be thoroughly humbled until he knows that his salvation is utterly beyond his own powers, devices, endeavors, will, and works, and that it depends entirely on the choice, will, and work of another, namely, of God alone. For as long as he is persuaded that he himself can do the least thing toward his salvation, he retains some self-confidence and does not altogether despair of himself, and therefore he is not humbled before God, but presumes that there is—at least he hopes or desires that there may be—some place, time, and work for him, by which he may at length attain to salvation. But when a man has no doubt that everything depends on the will of God, then he completely despairs of himself and chooses nothing for himself, but waits for God to work; then he has come close to grace, and can be saved.[5]

Here we reach the very heart of Luther's theology of justification by grace through faith, and we see that for the Reformer humility is synonymous with this saving faith. Oddly, Luther insists on the one hand that we are *made humble* by the Law, especially by the utter impossibility of keeping it; yet on the other hand we may come to desire this very humility.[6] Humanly speaking, being humbled might be mistaken for humiliation, but it's the very opposite. In fact, with humility we actually reclaim our full humanity in all of its down-to-earth integrity. Remember: the root of humility is *humus,* which means "of the earth." "We are meant to be human beings, not divine," comments Luther in his devotional writings.[7] "Therefore, the only complete righteousness is humility."[8]

Humbled, we at last become what we truly are called to be as creatures standing before their Creator. Life is no longer dominated by the performance of the false self. We begin to experience our true humanity as co-humanity and life itself as interdependent.

The Traces of Humility

Even though humility is not a human work or doing, it's still possible to observe the disposition of those who are humble and to note some of the earthly conditions that may make them humble. Mind you, the truly humble among us would find this discussion uninteresting or odd. They tend to be self-forgetful. If brought to their attention, even their humility would make them feel uneasy. And their unassuming temper would not be feigned.

First, we are made humble by *limitations*. Initially, reaching our limitations may be deflating, but then we can choose to "play within ourselves," as good athletes often put it. Rather than playing with complete, reckless abandon, the seasoned athlete learns to channel the passion of her life force into the routines, disciplines, and skills of her sport. Indeed, refusing to "play within ourselves" usually leads to losing. Limitations are "the givens" of life in this world. (As a young person I wanted to attend the Air Force Academy, but when the academy learned that I was color-blind, it turned me down, saying in so many words, "If you can't tell red from green, you might cross the wrong wires and blow something up.") To insist on playing any game with no "givens" at all is simply to opt out of the game altogether. Ask our first parents, Adam and Eve! Denying one's limits is magical thinking, imagining that I am "the exception" to the ordinary constraints of human life. In this regard, there's a huge difference between "pushing the limits" and refusing to acknowledge their existence. The absurd but dependable truth of a really good challenge in life is that we "push the limits" precisely by "playing within ourselves." (This in spite of Harry Potter's fabled gravity-defying game of quidditch.)

Second, "to be humble is *not to make comparisons*," as Dag Hammarskjöld writes in his diaries.[9] From the time we first go to school, we are taught to "compare and contrast." This analytic habit tends to infiltrate all of life, especially in our culture. Our society is above all a score-keeping society. As rabid competitors say, "Second place is the first loser." However, humble people seem to carry over into their everyday life less of this comparison bug. To borrow the language of addiction treatment, they seem to be less subject to the "external referent." Humble folk are not always looking up at the scoreboard during the game to see how other teams around the league are doing, nor do they do good deeds in order to elicit a "response" from those whom they favor—really, making others obliged and indebted. We sometimes say that people are "comfortable in their own skin." A humble person *unconsciously* exudes the character of Popeye the Sailor Man: "I am what I am and that's all that I am!"

Third, *knowing our place* makes us humble. Humility is finding this place to be just fine, thank you. The humble realize that they are not the only ones in the world, that they are part of something bigger than themselves. (Who has not looked up into the clear night sky, far from city lights, and experienced himself as a mere speck, but in that very gaze as being exalted above the confines of this world?) Humility is the knowledge of our interdependence with all things. It's an acknowledgment of our place in the web of life.

Leaders learn the humility of interdependence in many settings. One intense laboratory is the gathering in which you must deliberate and make decisions about someone's life and future. In my first year serving on our synod's candidacy committee, the group that examines candidates for ministry and decides whether they will be approved for the various stages of their training, I can remember sitting at the table and feeling that I had to have "the answer" or some profound insight about the profile of a particular candidate. When the issues regarding a person's readiness were confusing, or quite frankly beyond me, I felt ashamed that I couldn't resolve the dilemma for the committee. Gradually, I learned to rely upon and trust the wisdom of the group. Someone, or some combination of hunches and insights, would usually evoke an appropriate resolution—or, if not, an open acknowledgment that our deliberations had reached their limits and that the decision had to be postponed. That group wisdom outstrips all heroic individual wisdom is a lesson in the humility of interdependence.

When I think of the humility that comes from knowing one's place, I hear the music and lyrics of the old Shaker hymn:

> 'Tis the Gift to be Simple, 'Tis the Gift to be Free,
> 'Tis the Gift to come down where we ought to be.[10]

To summarize, Thomas Merton has observed, "Pride makes us artificial, and humility makes us real." Humility delights in the ordinary, Merton says:

> Such humility dares to be ordinary, and that is something beyond the reach of spiritual pride. Pride always longs to be unusual. Humility not so. Humility finds all its peace in hope, knowing that Christ must come again to elevate and transfigure ordinary things and fill them with His glory.[11]

In the rough-and-tumble of parish practice, leaders may be forgiven most things, except not being genuine. As a way of professional life, we may "fake it" for years, and we may even be rewarded by the ecclesiastical system, but unless the particular ministry site is unhealthy to the core, the sham leader will eventually be "found out." Yet humility is not a demeaning judgment about, but rather a truthful estimation of, ourselves. Humility and authenticity are one. Humility is "keeping it real."

The preaching life brings with it the temptation to fakery. What preacher has not felt an inner compulsion, an inner "must," "have to," or "should," to entertain the troops so that they don't fall asleep? After all, in our culture boredom is the eighth deadly sin. So we train ourselves to find a "hook" for our sermon, whether or not one exists. We obsess about illustrations instead of surrendering ourselves to the scriptural text—all in the name of professional craft. In candid moments with our soul, we yearn to let the Word take us where it will, and if in the process something amusing or colorful occurs to our fevered brains, fine. We long for the integrity to let gospel matters speak for themselves. We pray to keep it real.

Perhaps the most eloquent modern description of personal humility is found in the diaries of Dag Hammarskjöld. The full passage from which I took the earlier citation is this often-quoted text from *Markings*:

> Humility is just as much the opposite of self-abasement as it is of self-exaltation. To be humble is *not to make comparisons*. Secure in its reality, the self is neither better nor worse, bigger nor smaller, than anything else in the universe. It *is*— is nothing, yet at the same time one with everything. It is in this sense that humility is absolute self-effacement.
>
> To be nothing in the self-effacement of humility, yet, for the sake of the task, to embody *its* whole weight and importance in your bearing, as the one who has been called to undertake it. To give to people, works, poetry, art, what the self can contribute, and to take, simply and freely, what belongs to it by reason of its identity. Praise and blame, the winds of success and adversity, blow over such a life without leaving a trace or upsetting its balance.
>
> Towards this, so help me, God.[12]

"My dear boy, I was practicing self-effacement before you were even thought of."

The problem with this brief sketch of the shape of humility is that it bespeaks a utopian ideal. Because of the perversity of our human nature, we seem to choose humility only, if at all, once we have been humbled, perhaps even humiliated. If we are left to our own devices, humility, like faith, seems a sucker's bet. As heartfelt as Hammarsköld's testimony is, for instance, it seems to me unreal in its aspiration. The odds that I might be given the gift of "absolute self-effacement" are remote indeed! True humility is cruciform. Thus, any humility we may possess by accident of birth and natural temperament is fleeting. At the cross God finally reconciles humankind to the dignity of its allotted place as a covenant partner and co-creator. Humility now is faith's embrace of our rank as junior co-workers of God.

Leadership Paradox: Humility and Stubborn Resolve

Cross-shaped leaders are marked by personal humility. This observation is often lost on groups and organizations—with churches being the most gullible—that are desperate for order and "the answers" to their corporate dilemmas.

The eminent management researcher Warren Bennis declared, "The manager does things right; the leader does the right thing."[13] I've always thought that "the right thing" he refers to isn't so much something a person *does* as what a person *is*. Trusted leaders are humble yet strong-willed. Doing the right thing on a regular basis requires of the leader not master plans, but a paradoxical blend of humility and old-fashioned, stubborn resolve. As we shall see in the next chapter, having a vision is irrelevant unless people first buy into the leader herself. Visions are not self-recommending or self-authenticating apart from established relationships and partnerships. In this regard, the humility of the leader, the knowledge that she is not in it only for herself, is as crucial for the mission as her expertise and vision. Humility is virtually synonymous with the intangibles of character and integrity.

The most surprising conclusion of Stanford researcher Jim Collins's groundbreaking study about companies that have made the transition from "good to great," and have sustained their performance over the long haul, concerns the kind of CEOs they seem consistently to have. Such leaders, Collins concludes, invariably function with an odd combination of humility and doggedness. They seem to have very few ego needs; they do not seek the limelight, nor are they worried about who gets credit for what. Often, they are all but faceless to the public, known only by industry insiders. They tend not to go on talk shows or to produce "inspiring" business autobiographies. They direct their professional energy and effort exclusively toward the mission.[14]

This kind of leader is a rare breed. From a secular standpoint, the only thing to which I can compare this leadership profile comes from ancient wisdom traditions:

> *When the Master governs, the people*
> *are hardly aware that he exists. . . .*
> *The Master doesn't talk, he acts.*
> *When his work is done,*
> *the people say, "Amazing:*
> *we did it, all by ourselves!"*
>
> —TAO TE CHING[15]

Of this kind of leadership we can rightly say that *the doer disappears into the deed*. It's like great service at a restaurant—whether it's the local greasy spoon or the city's equivalent of the Four Seasons—in which the dining experience unfolds with almost no awareness of the comings and goings of the staff. Its efforts are submerged into the proceedings. Of course, such self-effacement is an ideal. Leaders of this stripe arise only once in a great while. And then we wonder whether this quality is the result of nature or nurture. My own sense is that these leaders are more "made" than "born." In the political arena, one thinks of a unique person like Harry Truman, who seems to have had few obvious ego needs, but who was dogged in the performance of his duty amid crisis and controversy, and who, when his time in office was done, went home to Missouri to lead an outwardly modest life.

Observation suggests that people have to undergo a sufficient amount of hardship, and to incorporate it into their personhood in a healthy manner, if they are to be shaped into high-functioning leaders whose only passion is the mission and the cause. When we say that someone is "integrated" in his or her personal development, this is what we have in mind. To be sure, it would be strange indeed if such a person had no natural endowments or talents at all; on the other hand, it would be stranger still if this individual had not been through some "refiner's fire" of life experience that had reshaped her and her talents. In the end, true leaders are cross-shaped.

There's no exact calculus here, then. Those who have "been through the mill" are perhaps more likely than others to learn humility. Once I attended a meeting that included newer clergy and church workers as well as some of us who were long in the tooth. Before the meeting, we talked about how to get over the tendency to take things personally. A new leader asked, "How do you do that?" An older pastor said things like, "There's really no formula except to go through the blame cycle enough times that it finally sinks in that it's not about you." "Yes," said another, "you have to get beat up enough times that you simply get over yourself." In this regard, leaders of the cross are most certainly made not by what they're born to, but by what they die to. Humility is not a natural virtue but a gift of faith from the one "who gives life to the dead and calls into existence the things that do not exist" (Rom. 4:17).

Pushing the Limits: On Having to Do Things You're No Good At

We began our discussion of humility by recounting how limitations may humble us. On this subject, there's a commonplace ministry experience I've found many of us don't want to talk about. Every day we have to do things we're no good at. Our prospects for improvement are slim, yet we're rightly called on to do them. Say what you want about our spiritual gifts working harmoniously within the context of a suitably matched ministry. I know of very few such matches that are truly made in heaven. At best, the match is always approximate.

Not every good preacher can organize her way out of a paper bag. This is the person of whom it was said, "She couldn't organize a two-car funeral procession." Not every good pastoral caregiver is eloquent in the pulpit. Not every manager who is good at "minding the store" knows why we do what we do except that it says so on the organizational flow chart. Our gifts differ, and so too do our liabilities and vulnerabilities. Part of the magical thinking that infects call committees and personnel committees is the expectation that the new hire or new call will include all of the strengths of the previous occupant of the position, plus those that were conspicuously absent. At some point, a reality check sobers everybody up. Then authentic and faithful ministry can begin.

Let me illustrate. In my early ministry years, I called a pastor friend who lived in another part of the country. We had been college roommates.

"So, how's it going?" I asked him.

"OK, I guess," he said, "but I'm really struggling with my preaching. It's hard."

"How do you live with this predicament," I asked, "since preaching is something that hangs over our heads almost every week? And after all, our tradition is big on proclamation."

"I don't really know," he said with his singsong Wyoming drawl. Frankly, his response made me worry for his personal well-being. I never stopped to consider the big picture of his giftedness that stood him in good stead with his congregation.

It's been over twenty-five years since we had that moment of long distance truth-telling. Not long ago my friend came through town, and we had a brief reunion. He's still in the mainstream of parish ministry. His self-confessed professional limitations, true or not, have not prevented him from being a faithful and effective pastor. Somehow his unique combination of gifts has enabled him to render great service to his community.

In recent years, I had a candid conversation with a prominent pastor who is head-of-staff in a high-profile congregation of a nearby synod. "John," he said, "I've always struggled with my visiting. I do it, and I work at it. But even after all these years of experience, when I'm sitting at someone's bedside in the hospital, I have trouble being present and paying attention the way they taught us in clinical pastoral education." Again, these particular limitations have in no way prevented him from rendering distinguished service.

Now, of course, what you want to know is what I'm willing to admit I'm no good at. Moreover, I presume you'd like me to do so in a way that does not cleverly redound to my credit. OK, what I'm no good at is asking people to do things, or as we sugarcoat it in the church, "recruiting and equipping for ministry." What the better angels of ministry call "empowering others," I often experience as plain old chasing and begging. I know better. But spiritual entrepreneurship is not my forte. Just as my late father was never that good at selling insurance—Willy Loman from *Death of a Salesman* and the play *Glengarry Glen Ross* have always haunted me—I could never sell all my "Scout-O-Rama" tickets door-to-door without my sister Jane's help. The equipping of the saints is a noble business but not one for which the Spirit has specially endowed my person and work. Yet the parish has every right to expect of me a minimum level of performance even in these areas.

At this point in the discussion, what we church professionals usually do is to say that if only we could get a fix on our inventory of spiritual gifts and then match it up with the missional needs of the right ministry setting, all would run smoothly. Or we speak with hope of continuing-education plans and covenants that might overcome our ministry deficits. We invent language about "growing edges."

What we won't do, however, is to admit that we may be at the end of our rope and dangling by a professional thread. After all, it's important to stand tall as a "visionary leader." (We'll have more to say about that leadership dogma in the next chapter.) Were it not for our limitations ("the good, the bad, and the ugly"), though, would we have *any* qualifications for ministry? The old medieval hymn *Felix culpa* ("Oh, Happy Fault!") comes to mind. What if the beginning of wisdom, and for that matter, the beginning of effective and faithful ministry, is to confess that ministry is quite simply impossible? And what if this is absolutely *not* an excuse, *not* a clever lowering of expectations that allows us to avoid giving it the good old college try? What if it's simply the *truth*? And what if embracing this truth is not only the beginning of wisdom, but also the beginning of faithful and effective leadership?

Sooner or later a Christian worker has to face the reality that ministry itself is an impossible possibility—not because it is so professionally complex and demanding, or because she doesn't have all the right gifts, or even because her congregation isn't, as they say, "healthy," but rather because what God asks of the world—and what we are charged to proclaim—is something about which the world quite simply freaks out: *dying in order to live.* Nobody wants to die to self. In the same way, dying to our well-laid ministry plans calls for *trust* that there's new life on the other side of their demise.

One of the questions we may ask seminarians at the several stages of their candidacy process is this: "What does Jesus's death and resurrection mean to you? What should it mean for the life and mission of the church?" Sometimes we get a dissertation of bookish proportions. Often we get a moving testimony about heaven and the afterlife. These are important and revealing moments.

What is uncommon, though, is the budding leader who says something like this: "You know, Jesus's death and resurrection should mean that we Christians are willing to let some of our ways die so that we may more faithfully answer God's call and serve others. If we actually live by the promise of the cross, maybe we can let go of our set ways of doing everything. Because of Easter and the promise of the resurrection, maybe, just maybe, the future of our church is not closed but open."

Humility leads to this down-to-earth approach to ministry. "Downward mobility" it's sometimes called. Simone Weil calls humility "the freely accepted movement toward the bottom."[16] Count yourself lucky if you happen to work with a tested leader of this stripe.

Looking back on what Pastor Kennedy proclaimed at the graduation, I think the graduates would surely hear it differently today than they did on that hot, humid day. Then it was "fair warning." Perhaps it was a good preacher's throwing down the gauntlet of the Law to soften up his targets for the Gospel onslaught to follow.

One thing is pretty certain: he went on to proclaim boldly the good news from 1 Peter that God "will exalt you in due time," because "he cares for you" (1 Pet. 5:6–7). The comfort and consolation of the gospel broke over the sweltering assembly like a tidal wave of grace. Shades of Martin Luther's testimony from the year before his death: "Here I felt that I was altogether born again and had entered paradise itself through open gates."[17]

Summary

We live in a culture of narcissism, where people careen between an inflated and a deflated self. Much of our life force is directed toward managing our image. Creating the right impression is the cottage industry of our soul. It's called "impression management" by those who treat diseases of addiction. Being real, neither more nor less than who we are, is a great and precious gift. Humility is that gift by which we are real. It's at the core of cross-shaped leadership.

1.   Humility, then, is not a human virtue but a gift of God. It is synonymous with faith. Humility is the outward face worn by faith.

2.   We are *made humble* by the knowledge of our human limitations, by an awareness of our interdependence with all of life, and by our inability to do what God wills and commands. Humility is cruciform.

3.   Humility is the promise, though not the fulfillment, of a comparison-free life. True humility is the gift of self-acceptance.

4.   Personal and corporate humility authenticates the mission of the church.

5.   Humility enables and empowers leaders to persevere in their mission.

✾ Questions for Discussion and Reflection

1.   Read the story of the Pharisee and the tax collector in Luke 18:9–14. Then read the great hymn to Christ in Philippians 2:1–11. On a scale of one to ten, with one being the least and ten being the most, how intense is your desire to receive credit for what you do for others? Are there situations in which this tendency is more pronounced?

2.   Read C. S. Lewis's classic description of humility in his popular *Screwtape Letters* (New York: Macmillan, 1977), pages 62–63. How does the devil play mind games with our desire to be humble? Why does the devil want us to be proud of being humble?

3.   Why is it easier for many people to confess their sins in bars instead of in churches?

4.   How can we reconcile our understandable wish to have our congregation make itself known in its community with the call to humility of life?

THE REVEREND
ANSWER PERSON
Closet Atheist

Blessed are they who do not have to impress others by showing how smart they are. —Christoph Blumhardt[1]

Great vision without great people is irrelevant. —Jim Collins[2]

Asbury sat up and thrust his thudding head forward and said, "I didn't send for you. I'm not answering any questions. You're not my doctor. What's wrong with me is way beyond you."

"Most things are beyond me," Block said. "I ain't found anything yet that I thoroughly understood," and he sighed and got up.
—Flannery O'Connor ("The Enduring Chill")[3]

You mean you're only now realizing that there are no answers?
—Chuang Tzu[4]

"Hey, Reverend, wait up," the voice called out from about half a block ahead of him. *Oh no,* Pastor Dave thought to himself, *all I wanted was a peaceful walk around the block.* It was clear, however, that Walter wasn't going to let him take his mid-afternoon break from the office in peace. He wasn't a member of the congregation. Still, you couldn't always avoid him.

When Walter approached him, Pastor Dave said, "Hi, Walter, how are you?"

"Fine," said Walter. "But, say, I was just wondering, why didn't Jesus condemn slavery?"

Oh no, Pastor Dave groaned inwardly. *What's this about? Do I really have to answer such a lame question? Besides, I have no idea why Jesus didn't condemn slavery.*

"Gee, I don't know, Walter. What do you think?"

"Well," he said, "*you're* the expert. I thought you'd know."

"I'm sorry, but I don't know the answer to that one, really."

Walter wouldn't let up. "I just thought you were the expert. I've asked this question many times over the years, but no one, not even the professors from the colleges around here, can give me an answer."

Cornered as he was at the intersection, all the Reverend could think to say was, "Maybe Jesus expected us to speak out about the issue on his behalf. You know, WWJD, 'What would Jesus do'?" Although he thought this was a pretty shrewd answer, it was clear that Walter wasn't impressed. Finally—and mercifully for both of them—they said good-bye and went their separate ways.

Now, of course, the armchair pastoral counselor in the Reverend hinted that what Walter really wanted had nothing to do with his question about Jesus, the Bible, and slavery. There was always—he knew this from frequent encounters—something else behind his questions. Usually it was simply about getting some attention. On this sunny afternoon, however, the Reverend was in no mood to try to read the pastoral tea leaves. Instead, another train of thought was triggered.

Why do I have to be an expert at all? Does that somehow justify my existence? Is having the answers proof that the church did the right thing in making me a pastor? What if I have to admit that often I really don't know? Does that make me bad, defective, or unworthy? In comparison to what?

The "Answer Man"

One of the things we've learned from people in the recovery and twelve-step movements is that a common trait of people with diseases of addiction is the compulsion always to be right. An addict desperately needs to be perfect; always being in the know is one way he gets his "fix." An air of fear and taboo surrounds the admission, "I don't know." It lies in the Forbidden Zone of life. Mistakes are unforgivable. And feelings of shame and low self-worth are the root of it all.

Our society displays all the symptoms of addiction.[5] The contemporary cult of the expert is but one indicator. Experts are the new priestly class of our culture. We speak in hushed tones of the information superhighway as if it were the path of righteousness. The old adage attributed to Mark Twain, "To a man with a hammer, the whole world looks like a nail," has as its modern parallel: "To a man with a computer, the whole world looks like data"[6] (though raw and undigested!).

Recently, a consultant who had been working with our church staff made me aware of my need always to be right. "What you have to realize about John," he said to our staff in a session, "is that half the time he doesn't know what he's doing!" At first I was startled and hurt by this pronouncement. Yet he went on to say, "But that's okay, John. You don't always *have to* know the answers. Give it a rest. It doesn't matter." "Yes, John," chimed in a colleague. "I can't bring up any topic you haven't read at least three or four books about. I'm sick of it."

Gradually, I have been trying to let go of this neurotic need to know. It's not easy, though. Expectations and pressure from others to be an authority feed into my own compulsion to "know it all." Years ago I had an interview with the bishop of a large metropolitan area. He wanted to meet with me before sending my name to the call committee of one of his congregations. In the feedback period at the end of the interview, he chided me for coming across with too much of a humble, Midwestern "aw-shucks" manner. "That will never work in this city," he declared. "You've got to put yourself out there." And indeed, he was right. The ensuing interview with the call committee—conducted in the plush offices of a law firm that occupied four floors of a skyscraper—was polite, calculated, and subtly condescending. *Don't call us; we'll call you.*

How degrading that in our day even knowledge, which God intends as a gift (consider how the Bible, especially a book like Proverbs, extols "wisdom"), can become someone's "drug of choice." Instead of seeking wisdom as a basis for truth, honesty, and excellence, we may use it subtly to show off, to dominate, or merely to manage impressions. Always having the answers makes us the keeper of secrets that others—and of course, this is the point—*don't* have. So if I have such esoteric knowledge, I must be special—right?

Yet a mysterious peace steals over us when we finally abandon our compulsion to have the answers. We fall into an uncharacteristic silence and let things be. At a congregational meeting some years ago, I experimented with silence by deliberately saying nothing for the entire ninety minutes after I gave the opening prayer. To be sure, I received strange looks and inquiries about my health ("Is John OK?" asked the associate pastor's spouse). But I resolved that unless the gospel itself was in jeopardy, I would shut up. Miraculously, the people found their own answers, and did so quite well, thank you. Never mind the quest for a "visionary leader."

I hope that I'm done being the Reverend Answer Person. Probably not, though. After all, only the Holy Spirit can persuade us to trust that the Holy Spirit actually runs the church—and to know the God-breathed difference between such trust and the avoidance of legitimate responsibility and action. Knowing the difference between what work belongs to us and what work does not belong to us is the answer to a prayer for wisdom. It is a cross-shaped wisdom that comes only as a gift in praying, "Come, Holy Spirit!"

First Covenant (Partnership) . . . Then Vision

Have you noticed how fashionable, indeed, chic, it has become in the life of the church to talk about "vision"? For some time, this vogue has made me uneasy, but I have been unsure why. It could be the slipperiness of the language itself.

Sometimes talk of vision means something as simple as a person's ability to look ahead. It's old-fashioned foresight, or perhaps the tendency to perceive the "big picture" of situations before we zero in on the details. This is vision as a verb, vision as "visioning." We might well question why something so commonplace as foresight deserves such a grandiose label as "vision," but then language inflation, the language of self-importance, is epidemic in today's organizational life. Then there's vision as a noun: here vision may mean a plan or an idea. "What's your vision?" means "What's your scheme or plan?" Or it could mean, "What's 'the answer'?" Of course, the ultimate in vision talk is vision as a kind of dream. And when people get really desperate, this can cross over into no-holds-barred fortune-telling. Now the Reverend Answer Person becomes the Reverend Nostradamus!

The language of the visionary, or seer, in other words, leads us onto the holy ground of current leadership dogma. If leaders claim to have a "vision for mission," they may be credited with mystical access to the glory road of organizational rebirth. The reputed, or longed-for, visionary leader may be exalted as a mastermind whose penetrating gaze discovers the Holy Grail of his "purpose-driven" renewal schemes. (Do you remember a recent presidential campaign in which one candidate seemed to begin every sentence with the words, "Now, I have a plan"?) It's uncanny how strategic planning can sound almost messianic in its zeal, not unlike Israel's waiting for the righteous king who will solve the people's problems and bring back their storied prosperity and influence. Vision talk is heady stuff, indeed, sounding forth like thunder and lightning from Mount Sinai.

In such lofty scenarios, vision often ends up being not what it is in the Bible (the living voice of the Word heard in the here-and-now of the community's unfolding proclamation) or in the great mystical traditions (in which God *utters the believer* like a partial thought of God's own self), but rather a thinly disguised quest for an "answer man." How many desperate congregations charge the call committee with the task of going out and finding such a visionary leader? And how many of them mean not someone *who will partner with them* in hearing the gospel and in facing up to the brutal facts about their life together in community, but rather someone who has put together, and is shopping around, an ecclesiastical "business plan"? Mission happens when "vision" begins to mean something more than "the answer," when a living Voice enters the hearing of people in their "life together." Then it may come to pass that, as Dietrich Bonhoeffer foretells it, "The early morning mists of dreamy visions are lifting," and "the bright day of Christian community dawns."[7]

One of the astonishing, and frankly sobering, conclusions of Jim Collins's groundbreaking research into the characteristics of organizations that have made the transition from "good to great," and have stayed there over the long haul, is that the leaders of such groups never lead with the question of vision—the "what" question, as Collins calls it—but always with the question of people, the "who" question. For these leaders, whom they want to work with and the gifts they bring into a partnership and, just as important, whom they *do not* want to work with, precede even the question of what business they might go into! Before they even know what widget they're in business to make, they know first of all *whom* they've always been dying to work with, never mind on what. This approach to planning is not a matter of personality but a discernment of giftedness and the possibilities of building working partnerships. Only then follows the question of vision. It's a function of the covenants among these people; it arises from and remains grounded in such partnerships, never becoming untethered as some brilliant "silver bullet" idea or, worse, some top-down strategic plan. As Collins puts it, "who is on the bus" comes even before "where the bus is going."[8]

When organizations lead with the question "What's your vision?" instead of "Who are you (and who are we in this place)?" they are very much at risk of developing a leadership style Collins calls "the hero with a thousand helpers."[9] This is the CEO or charismatic leader who ends up going on talk shows and promoting her business autobiography with the story of how she brought the XYZ Corporation back from the brink of ruin.

When we grant that the "who question" (people in partnership) must always come before the "what question" (vision), however, then "the answers" arise from genuine community discernment. The Christian tradition calls this discernment *viva vox evangelii* ("the living voice of the gospel"). What the theological tradition means is that the Word that comes to us in Scripture is not a dead word on the printed page of a book but a living Word that leaps off the page, the dynamic bombshell of a reality ("words of eternal life") that *happens to us* in the present moment of faith. And the Word explodes in our midst because God is the living God, Jesus is risen and in our midst, and the Spirit therefore continues to unfold the meaning of the scriptural text in the here and now of the assembly. In this way, as the great hymn puts it, when "I sing the new, new song," I am in fact singing "the old, old story that I have loved so long."

Vision, then, originates not in seeing but in hearing a voice, the living voice of the good news sounding forth within, and from, the assembly. Theologically, vision talk can be ventured only in the context of the church at prayer. Vision is a product of collective listening for the *viva vox evangelii.* That is why worship in word and sacrament isn't just one ministry among others (the work of "the worship team"); rather it's the ministry of ministries. It fuels learning, witness (evangelism), servant life, and support (stewardship). Vision isn't something we *have*; it's a reality that *has us.* It's cross-shaped. Pragmatically, it has us by our constantly asking questions, by our establishing a climate of dialogue, an environment of call and response.

The Question of Questions

What does the Bible have to say about vision? It's tempting to seek the answer by taking out that trusty old Bible study tool, the concordance, and looking up all the passages that use the word "vision"—and then conducting some kind of statistical analysis. Or we might go further and dissect some of the classic vision/call stories, such as Isaiah in the Temple (Isa. 6), Ezekiel's wheel within a wheel (Ezek. 1:16), or the valley of dry bones (Ezek. 37), Jesus on the Mount of Transfiguration (Matt. 17), the women at the garden tomb (Matt. 28), Paul on the road to Damascus (Acts 9), or the Pentecost story in which the Spirit promises that "your young men will dream dreams, and your old men will see visions" (Acts 2). Well, you get the idea.

But let's approach this question a bit differently by noting some overarching biblical themes. First, long ago it was recognized that there is a tension in the Scriptures between "seeing" and "hearing."[10] This is especially true in the Hebrew Scriptures. The classic passage is Moses hiding his face in the cleft of the rock as Yahweh passes by (Exod. 33). Because God is "wholly other," and thus holy beyond compare, humans aren't allowed to behold Yahweh face to face. To gaze directly upon Yahweh would be to die. But humans can listen to and hear God's voice and call, whether from the burning bush of Moses or in the "sound of sheer silence" that enveloped Elijah (1 Kings 19:12). St. Paul inherits this strand of the biblical tradition when he declares that "faith comes from what is heard" (Rom. 10:17).

Second, in the Christian Scriptures, one of the consequences of sin is that creation's original transparency has been marred. St. Paul famously declared, "Now we see in a mirror, dimly, but then we will see face to face" (1 Cor. 13:12). Apparently this passage refers to how mirrors were made in the first century, fashioned from polished metal, and thus limited in the clarity of their reflection. More to the point, Paul tells the church at Rome that God's will in creating the world was that creation would be transparent to human vision. God's desire was that humans would "see through" creation and behold God. But—and for Paul this "but" is the first great crossroad in our relationship with God—human sin has marred this transparency of creation (Rom. 1:18–32). We no longer "see through" creation directly to God. Sin has given us cataracts, or worse, macular degeneration! So, in this life we walk by faith (which is a matter of hearing), not sight (a matter of vision).

Third, the more we read and listen to Matthew, Mark, Luke, and John, the more we notice a recurring question people ask about Jesus: *Who, then, is this?* "Who is this who even forgives sins?" (Luke 7:49). "Who then is this, that even the wind and the sea obey him?" (Mark 4:41). From prison John the Baptist asks, "Are you the one who is to come, or are we to wait for another?" (Matt. 11:3). "But who do you say that I am?" Jesus himself asks the disciples (Matt. 16:15). "Who is this?" the crowds ask as he enters Jerusalem in procession (Matt. 21:10). "Who is this Son of Man?" the crowd at Bethsaida asks (John 12:34). "Are you the King of the Jews?" Pilate finally asks (John 18:33). For all the diversity in their portrayals of Jesus, the Gospels seem incessantly driven by this "who" question, the question of Jesus's identity.

Even the "vision" of the kingdom of God that dominates the parables in Matthew, Mark, and Luke is linked inescapably with the "who" of Jesus in his person and work. The kingdom vision is a function of Jesus, not the other way around. Jesus is the bringer of the kingdom; the kingdom is not the bringer of Jesus. The God who is "with us" (Matt. 1:23) in the manger is an "in the flesh" (incarnate) Savior, not an ideology, an agenda, or a program. In the kingdom, too, first comes who, then what!

It has been said, "People buy into the leader, then the vision."[11] This, I take it, is not a remark about the genius or forceful personality of leaders, but rather something deeper about the proven trustworthiness of the leader in covenant partnership with others. The Hebrew Scriptures call this relational way of being *hesed,* or "steadfast love" (Exod. 34:6–7). Before leaders of the cross offer answers to anything, they practice *hesed* in mutual listening for the living voice of the gospel. They ask questions. They are steadfast yet responsive. They are able to restrain themselves from giving their own blueprint for mission. They trust that the way forward in mission is there for the hearing of all in the assembly.

God Hidden, God Revealed

Martin Luther's distinction between the "hidden God" and the "revealed God" theologically grounds genuine vision talk, which arises from the assembly's listening to the living voice of the gospel. The hidden God is God in God's self, God apart from all the earthly ways and events and circumstances and people and places through which God chooses to make known God's self. The hidden God is God without any creaturely intermediary, God in God's naked being.[12] Until we "get to heaven," as they say, we have no access to this God, what St. Paul calls seeing God "face to face." Vision is for the world to come.

Instead, now in this earthly life "we see in a mirror, dimly." We encounter God only *indirectly, through* the things and events and people of this world. And not just among wonderful and lovely things, but even, and perhaps especially, among unlovely and troublesome things and circumstances. Indeed, precisely there, in the least likely places, in failure and suffering and dying and loss, God is trying to get us to pay special attention to God's presence and call. This is the heart of theology of the cross.

Contrast this mediated presence with the insatiable desire in the history of religion to encounter God *apart from all mediation,* apart from all earthly incarnation ("in the flesh") as go-between.

This is the impulse that leads to every cult. We may plead that all we want is to be "uplifted" when we go to church, but this craving for, and even the collecting of, religious experiences quickly turns into the Golden Calf of much contemporary spirituality with its utopian yearning for paradise on earth.

For Luther, "true theology and recognition of God are in the crucified Christ."[13] God reveals God's self not by lifting us out of this world, but by hiding in its midst, and exactly in the thick of things as they have been disfigured by human sin. In Christ, God does not bypass fallen human existence but enters into it as God's dwelling. Our "vision" of God, therefore, shines forth from an unwelcome baby in a manger, a criminal on the cross, and a body in the grave. Knowing God in this way is a "knowing" in the biblical sense of knowing: not a theory or even information, much less a blueprint, but rather *God's* act of radical and intimate trust. We *know* only as we are *known.* Our knowing isn't something we do, but something we undergo. Our knowing is cruciform, partial and patiently awaiting the promise of its completion not in this life but in the next. So, too, any vision for mission is cruciform. We don't "lift up" the vision; it calls out from the depths of the assembly's often tangled existence. True vision is always blurred and unfinished, and it emerges from below, not above. Visionary leaders are made—indeed, forged—by their solidarity with the Body's suffering in the depths of its crucified Self.

Church Workers as Closet Atheists

Cross-shaped leaders are marked by trust that God is the same in himself as God reveals himself *to* us and *for* us. As we look upon what Luther called "the friendly face of Christ," we see the fullness of God. There's nothing more to behold than this sight; there's nothing more behind or beyond this "vision" with which we need, or dare, concern ourselves.

For leaders to speculate beyond what God has chosen to reveal on the cross is to walk the path of the "closet atheist." The more prosaic way to sketch this leadership profile is to speak of what various people have called either "practical atheism" or "functional atheism."

The closet atheist is someone who protests that he has always believed in God, or at least a God of sorts, but who manages the nitty-gritty of his life and its affairs *as though there were no God.* You don't have to be an official atheist to be a closet one. All you need do is to live focused on me and my and mine, or worry yourself to death about picking up after the whole world. The motto, the creed, of closet atheists is "If I don't do it, nobody will." Their (more often than not, "our") creed is a self-fulfilling prophecy with rock-solid proof from everyday life.

In theory, closet atheists believe in God; in practice, they trust nobody beyond the self. They are prisoners of mistrust. They judge God's providential care to be for simpletons. A slow spiritual death is sure to follow for those who are convinced that others can't be trusted to keep their commitments. Again, visit with those in the recovery and twelve-step movements for a graphic description of, and witness to, the death of faith (trust) that occurs when addicts are, as members say, "really into their disease."

For those in leadership, this propensity is perhaps the greatest of all occupational hazards. Slowly, cunningly, the Father of Lies whispers to the leader, or to anyone who has responsibility in the lives of others (try parenthood on for size!), *You must always have the answer. After all,* you're *the pastor [or parent]. If you don't do it, nobody will.* And how can one argue with such perverse logic?

I've not had many scary moments in ministry, but one that is still fresh in my mind is the occasion some years ago when a church elder criticized me for my supposed neglect of a lapsed church member. (For me the issue wasn't the merit of his charge, for he might well have been right, but rather that he waited for me to go out of town to voice the accusation at a meeting.) When I challenged him about his actions, in a private meeting with two other elders, he said to me, "John, what you have to realize is that for many people the pastor *is* the church."

At that moment, the hair stood up on the back of my neck, and I blurted out, "Yes, and Stalin *was* Russia [he was called 'The Great Man'], and Mussolini *was* Italy [remember, he 'made the trains run on time']. What you're saying really scares me. Whatever happened to 'mutual' ministry and the 'priesthood of all believers'?"

More to the point: Christ *is* the church; it's *his* Body, not ours. Admittedly, as many as 15 percent of those within any congregation would instinctively agree that the pastor *is* the church. A leader of the cross will be vigilant, however, about the dangers of this messianic projection.[14]

However, another kind of atheism may visit the leader: the desolate not-knowing that attends a personal crisis of faith. Timothy Wengert tells the poignant story of a gifted seminary student who undergoes such a crisis. He asks whether her struggle with belief in God disqualifies her from public service in the church.[15] One hardly knows how to answer this question.

On the one hand, whom would you rather have as your leader—someone who has struggled with faith or someone for whom faith has always come easily? As Wengert says, "Here was someone whose best qualification as a pastor came in the form of atheism, yet she could hardly tell a soul."[16] (The real problem is not, finally, our *being* atheists, but our having to live the lie that we are not assaulted by doubts.) On the other hand—and as I said above—being a "wounded healer" is great as long as some significant healing has occurred and scar tissue has built up. Remember: there's a big difference between wounded healers and bleeding ones!

Resident Theologian?

I have poked fun at the image of the Reverend Answer Person. Please don't take this as a call for anti-intellectualism or as a suggestion that no professional preparation is needed for ministry. Brains are useful. God makes brains, and, so far as I can tell, the Creator is rather fond of our gray matter. The real issue, of course, is not one of IQ but rather the love of learning. People benefit when leaders are learners.

An image of the pastor currently popular in seminary circles is that of the "resident theologian." When this is meant to portray the minister as the reference department of the church library, or as a theological resource, consultant, or expert, we have only scratched the surface of what it truly means to be a theologian in residence. Clergy are called to be *working* theologians in residence.

What does this mean, or rather, how is this role played out in parish practice?

Consider this example. The new pastor learns that the annual church bazaar is held not to benefit a charitable mission but to pay for the heat and light bills and other current expenses from the congregation's budgetary shortfall. She tries to remind people that our money doesn't really belong to us, and that it may well be "ill-gotten gains" when used for these self-serving purposes. She becomes the target of grumbling and complaining and momentarily considers "making a whip of cords" (John 2:15), but her cooler head prevails, and her firm but respectful stand results in a working consensus. Eventually, the people come around and agree to hold the bazaar for community outreach and fellowship.

Being a theologian in residence, then, is not about moonlighting as a scholar or even being the "master teacher" at the adult forum, but about *functioning* theologically in the give-and-take of parish practice, decision making, and planning. Resident theology is a God-centered habit of mind and heart that kicks into gear when the community has lost its way or is trying to find a way forward in mission. The role of the resident theologian is to throw a gospel light on the purposes and plans and practices that, both daily and long-term, make up our parish life in mission. The cross-shaped theologian always speaks this gospel: our lives are in God's hands—really!

The acid test for a working theologian in residence often comes in dealing with money. Few issues, perhaps not even sexuality, are as "hot-button" as that of money, including its uses and misuses, and the anxiety over its scarcity. In confidential pastoral conversation, people will divulge the most salacious details of their marital infidelities, addictions, and personal failings, but the last taboo is to tell you their annual income. In our society, there's no shame like the shame over work and money. If you want an entrée into the primal unconscious life of a group, simply ask for money. You may not like what you hear (the old maxim is that "the truth will set you free, but first it will make you miserable"), but you will find that the can of worms that has been opened is really a treasure trove of information vital for building working partnerships with the community.

A formal feasibility study that preceded a capital campaign our congregation conducted some years ago was revealing. The development firm we hired to help us carry out the campaign conducted in-depth, confidential interviews with sixty-five families of the congregation. The candid remarks about our proposed project revealed as much about the spiritual "state of the union" within our parish as any Bible study or group-therapy process could have. People said what they truly thought and felt about our common mission, their personal faith, and the state of parish relationships, including those with and within the staff.

At times, the study made for sober reading. Mostly, however, people told "the truth in love" (Eph. 4:15), and definite patterns emerged about the people's own "vision" for their life together in mission. The vision, or rather the *voice*, was not from above, but from below, buried amid the untidy circumstances of their life together. We came to realize that our task as leaders was that of listeners and interpreters for the sounds of the "passion" that we were all "suffering."

True resident theologians are leaders who have imbibed deeply of Luther's explanation of the First Commandment from *The Large Catechism*. They are instinctively on the lookout for signs of what the "whole heart clings and grasps" onto for its security, and therefore as its "god." They ask the assembly probing questions about where people place their trust and where their hearts "find refuge in all need."[17] Pastorally and theologically, they learn to dissect and to diagnose the chronic fear that surrounds such common statements as, "Faith doesn't pay the bills." Well, yes, it does. Faith isn't a magic charm, but faith is life in Christ—indeed, Christ *as* our life. In faith, the self has been crucified with Christ, so that the self's grasping insecurity no longer has demonic control of its life. Faith may not print money, but faith does free us to pay the bills.

The question for people of faith is always: Are we possessed by our possessions? Are we "had" by what we have? "Mammon," Luther remarks, "is the most common idol on earth." It is cunning and demonic in the power of its promises. Luther goes on: "Those who have money and property feel secure, happy, and fearless, as if they were sitting in the midst of paradise. On the other hand, those who have nothing doubt and despair as if they knew of no god at all." At every stage of life, mammon wears a new face, inspiring new fears. Says Luther: "This desire for wealth clings and sticks to our nature all the way to the grave."[18]

A resident theologian, therefore, is a general practitioner of ministry who has developed a habit of the heart that listens within the assembly for "anything on which your heart relies and depends, I say, that is really your God."[19] Moreover, the only antidote to the poison of the self's false gods is "the living voice of the gospel." And a strong dose of the true and good preaching of the Law, to borrow a phrase from Mary Poppins, "makes the medicine go down."

Summary

The following are some provisional conclusions about vision that are based on the pastoral experiences and reflections offered above.

First, cross-shaped leaders invest their primary energies and efforts in trust building and covenant making. They know that people must trust the leader, and one another, before they will endorse any vision. Before leaders are visionaries or seers, they are listeners and questioners in solidarity with the assembly. "Vocation does not come from willfulness. It comes from listening," asserts Parker Palmer.[20]

Second, authentic vision is not a master plan sold as an agenda; vision is rather the living voice of the gospel as it sounds forth within and from the assembly. It echoes not from above, but from below. The leader expects to behold the vision from within the chaos of the community's life together. And whatever her particular spiritual gifts may be, she commits to excellence in word and sacrament ministry.

Third, cross-shaped leaders pray for wisdom to know the difference between the work that does, and does not, fall to them in mutual ministry.

Fourth, cross-shaped leaders vigilantly observe and apply the First Commandment that the assembly is to have no other gods before it. And the leader is the first to repent of running after other gods, especially the god of self-sufficiency.

By the way, I still have no idea why Jesus didn't condemn slavery. (A scholar would probably tell us that it has something to do with social conditions in the ancient world, though I doubt that the Reverend's walking companion, Walter, would buy this theory, either.) But at a minimum, *I know that I don't know*, and, like the fear of the Lord, that may be the beginning of wisdom.

❖ Questions for Discussion and Reflection

1. Read these three texts about vision: Moses hiding in the cleft of the rock (Exod. 33:12–23); Jesus on the mountain of Transfiguration (Matt. 16:13–17:13); and the stoning of Stephen, the first Christian martyr (Acts 7:54–60). What factors that are a permanent part of our lives mean that our vision is always obscured? How is true vision cruciform?

2. When the way forward in mission is confusing and you must admit that you don't have the answer, what are some of the steps to take in getting unstuck? When is waiting helplessly OK for a time?

3. In the professional world of church leaders, what are some of the false gods that you are tempted to run after?

4. When was the last time you read a really "hard-core" book of theology and found that it either renewed or reinforced your sense of call and vocation in general?

LIFE TOGETHER
In Sickness and in Health

The Church is something like Noah's Ark. If it weren't for the storm outside, you couldn't stand the smell inside. —Late Medieval Manuscript[1]

Life seeks order, but it uses messes to get there. —Margaret J. Wheatley[2]

In a church that is almost dead or totally dead, people gossip about one another's weaknesses. There is little, if any, church discipline, and therefore no forgiveness either.
—J. Heinrich Arnold[3]

I called through your door,
"The mystics are gathering
in the street. Come out!"
"Leave me alone. I'm sick."
"I don't care if you're dead!
Jesus is here, and he wants
to resurrect somebody!"
—Jelaluddin Rumi[4]

S tan Laurel (of the comedy duo Laurel and Hardy) often said to Oliver Hardy, "Well, here's another fine mess you've gotten me into." Eventually, this complaint inspired the title of one of their movies: 1930's *Another Fine Mess*. In Frank Capra's 1939 classic drama *Mr. Smith Goes to Washington*, Jimmy Stewart, aka Mr. Smith, whose late father had been a crusading journalist and known as a champion of the underdog, tells the corrupt senior senator played by Claude Rains, "Lost causes are the only ones worth fighting for."

These are good expressions to help us make sense of the real world of parish practice. To all human appearances, it's a real mess, and a lost cause to boot, but once we accept this view, ministry gets a lot easier and more productive. So let's look at the mess and take up its lost cause, trusting that the creator God is trying to bring some life-giving order out of its chaos. After all, isn't finding new life in the middle of turmoil, suffering, and death the calling of a cross-shaped leader?

"Another Fine Mess"

Those first two weeks at Faith Church were a blur. No sooner had the new pastor settled into the office than he received a phone call from one of the victims and complainants of his predecessor's misconduct. Apparently she wanted to "check him out" to see if the next pastor would be any different from the predator who had come before him. Of course, the meeting took place in broad daylight and with the office doors wide open and plenty of human traffic in the church building.

But then she called him again the next week to report that someone whom she had briefly dated was stalking her. And since the stalker knew that she was a churchgoer, he had, she said, shown up in the church parlor on several recent Sundays. Pastor and congregant met again, this time with the chief of police, himself new to the community, and they spread out on the pastor's office floor the many threatening letters she had been sent by the suspected perpetrator. Eventually the stalker was arrested and taken to a mental-health facility. But the new pastor went home and said to his wife, "Maybe I should have thought twice about accepting the call here."

When we work in a setting where chaos and creepiness have reigned, there are pitfalls and lessons. The pitfalls and lessons are probably no different from those in "normal" settings, but they do become magnified. A congregation in recovery is a real proving ground for ministry practice in general. The "fine mess" we've gotten ourselves into teaches us to look at the unvarnished truth about our setting, and it also teaches us to trust the promise that some order, however hidden, is always trying to manifest itself within the mess. It's the Pentecost miracle of a restored, indeed reborn, faith community. It's the host of the "dry bones" standing upright and having flesh and sinews come upon them and the Spirit come from the four winds to resurrect the "whole house of Israel" (Ezek. 37). The calling of the leader is to *unabashedly proclaim the gospel, stand fast, pay attention, ask questions*—and to be disciplined in refusing to avoid reality. The scriptural promise that undergirds the cross-shaped leader's stance is the paradox St. Paul experienced in his own ministry: "So, I will boast all the more gladly of my weaknesses, so that the power of Christ may dwell in me. Therefore I am content with weaknesses, insults, hardships, persecutions, and calamities for the sake of Christ; for whenever I am weak, then I am strong" (2 Cor. 12:9b–10).

We've already mentioned the work of Jim Collins and his associates to identify the leadership factors that the most durable, high-functioning companies seem to have in common. Leaders tend to exhibit a paradoxical mixture of humility and stubborn resolve. Also, they rarely lead with the "what question," the question of vision, and more often begin with the "who question," the question of people in partnership. "Who's on the bus" comes before "where the bus is going."

But another major finding of this research is that the identified companies have leaders who resolutely look at "the brutal facts" of their current reality yet never lose faith in a positive end game.[5] There's no queasy avoidance, no sugarcoating, of reality. The wisdom of a Winston Churchill prevails: "There is no worse mistake in public leadership than to hold out false hopes soon to be swept away."[6] It would be a mistake to portray this counsel as being negative in contrast to being positive. It is in fact *beyond* positive and negative; it is simply real. It's about honesty. There's no better commentary on the ludicrousness of "positive thinking" in the Western psyche than Monty Python's anthem from *The Life of Brian* and the musical *Spamalot,* in which Jesus, the two thieves, and a host of others hanging on crosses sing, "Always look on the bright side of life!" (No lie: as a student pastor I actually had a supervisor tell me one day that when Jesus was hanging on the cross, he was a "winner." You can't make this stuff up.)

But notice another leadership paradox: those who steadfastly confront the brutal facts of their current reality maintain an unwavering faith that they can and will prevail in the end. However, they refuse to set any timetable. In faith, and for the long haul, they live the contradiction. The example Collins cites is that of Admiral James Stockdale, who spent eight years as a tortured prisoner in the infamous "Hanoi Hilton" during the Vietnam War. When asked why he and others made it out alive while still others did not, Stockdale said that they never lost faith that they would prevail in the end, yet they never allowed themselves to think things like, "I'll be home by Christmas" or "I'll be home by whenever." And when he was asked who didn't make it out alive, he said, "Oh, that's easy, the optimists."[7] They died of broken hearts.

Such tenacious faith that never denies the harshness, even brutality, of circumstances breathes a spirit that is stoic in its resolve. We do not recoil from chaos, confusion, and disorder, but rather trust that amid ruin and decay some emergent order is struggling to reveal itself. Perhaps the great German poet Rilke said it best: "It is clear that we must trust in what is difficult; everything alive trusts in it. . . . We know little, but that we must trust in what is difficult is a certainty that will never abandon us."[8] With much less drama, but in words based on scientific observation of living systems, management researcher Margaret Wheatley writes: "Life seeks order, but it uses messes to get there."[9] Cross-shaped leaders learn to stand fast and to pay attention to the "fine mess" in which they and the people find themselves. Their stance is far from heroic, nor is it taken up in splendid isolation; it is faith-based, that is, *theological* (God-centered) and collegial.

Marks of the Church: The God-Given Means of Cross-Shaped Leadership

One of the staples of theology of the cross is Martin Luther's insistence that we know God "under the form of opposites" (*sub contrario specie*) and that "A theology of the cross calls a thing what it actually is."[10] Here we come to the heart of Christian faith and the knowledge of God.

Luther's starting point is the New Testament (Heb. 11:1) definition of faith as having "to do with things not seen."[11] For our sake, and for the sake of faith, God hides in the middle of circumstances that seem contrary to the expected ways of a deity. God draws us to God not by escorting us out of this world, but by sending us back into the depths of our human condition with all its contradictions, brokenness, joys and sorrows, and successes and abject failures. This God is truly a "God with us," the one whose name is Immanuel. Luther writes in 1525:

> Hence in order that there may be room for faith, it is necessary that everything which is believed should be hidden. It cannot, however, be more deeply hidden than under an object, perception or experience which is contrary to it. Thus when God makes alive he does it by killing, when he justifies he does it by making men guilty, when he exalts to heaven he brings down to hell, as Scripture says, "The Lord kills and brings to life; he brings down to Sheol and raises up" (1 Sam. 2:6).[12]

Seven years earlier Luther had put it this way: "Although the works of God are always unattractive and appear evil, they are nevertheless eternal merits."[13] The crucified God judges not by appearances but by the reality beneath the appearances. This God is truly a God who "loves the unlovely" and thereby transforms and renews a lost creation.

Theology of the cross, then, says that we know God in the least likely places and ways: in chaos and turmoil and suffering and in the valley of the shadow of death. To pick up on the theme of this chapter's previous section, God reveals God's self amid "the brutal facts" of our personal and communal life. The true working of God is always unattractive to human sight. A theology of glory looks upon the brutal facts only with revulsion; a theology of the cross feels the birth pangs of a New Creation.

A *theologian* of the cross, Luther is adamant, beholds all the decay and ruin "and says what a thing actually is." By not turning away in revulsion or denial, she becomes a leader shaped by the cross, shaped by suffering divine things. Both her job description and required professional skills are to "say what a thing actually is." She is marked by a fierce dedication to reality for the health and well-being of the assembly.

For almost a generation now, the accepted professional framework for assessing churches' well-being has been one of "healthy" and "unhealthy" congregations. The health model, with its roots in biology and living systems, has been a useful and adaptable tool in parish practice. However, it rarely reaches—nor even claims to reach—the deep recesses of the community's self in which "the world, the flesh, and the devil" are at work. As I understand it, family systems theory, which does indeed attend to systemic anxiety, doesn't find it necessary to probe the unconscious life of individuals or groups to any great depth. This horizontal approach may increase its practicality, but to my mind it is also a limitation.

The "fine mess" or "brutal facts" of normal parish practice do yield, however, to what our faith tradition calls the "marks of the church." The "marks of the church" are the God-given means by which and with which the assembly and its leaders go about the task of "saying what a thing is." The marks of the church are a gift with which the community does God's reality check on itself.

The marks of the church didn't become a hot topic until the Protestant Reformation and the Roman Catholic Counter-Reformation that followed. Since everybody was feuding over whose church was the true church, lists of true church attributes were bound to be put forward. The so-called classical marks of the church were in fact buried in the ancient Nicene Creed: one, holy, catholic (universal), and apostolic. It wasn't until the nineteenth century, however, that Anglo-Catholics lifted them up as an explicit litmus test of orthodoxy!

Luther's earlier proposal, based on his reading of Scripture, included the following seven marks: the preached word of God; baptism; holy communion; the Office of the Keys (the use of absolution for sin); the Office of Ministry (the calling and consecrating of ministers); the public use of prayer, praise, and thanksgiving; and possession of the sacred cross (the experience of suffering in communal life). On the Catholic side of the fight after the Council of Trent (1545–1563), the theologian Robert Bellarmine (1542–1621) named fifteen marks! What distinguishes Luther's understanding is that for him "church" is, we might say, a verb, an event. The church is not the origin of the marks; the marks *originate* the church. And they do so in the here-and-now assembly of living people. The church is the happening of its marks.

My thesis here is that rightly understood, and integrated into the life of the assembly, these marks are the theological underpinning for the proper use of our clinical or managerial tools. The clinical and management models come and go, and although we should pay serious attention to these trusty tools (do go to the workshops), on their own they are not what gives life to the assembly of believers. They are expressions and applications of the marks of the church. They belong in the professional tool chest, but they are really adjuncts to the preaching, sacraments, prayer and spiritual direction, public offices, and absolution of sins.

It's no accident that Luther would name "possession of the sacred cross" as one of the marks of the church. This term refers not only to the suffering of the individual but also to the suffering of the community beleaguered from within and without. Luther's understanding went back to St. Augustine, who saw the church as a mixed membership of saints and sinners whose sorting out must await God's judgment alone at the end of time. Until then, the assembly endures "misfortune and persecution, all kinds of trials and evil from the devil, the world, and the flesh . . . by outward sadness, timidity, fear, outward poverty, contempt, illness, and weakness" to become like Christ, the head.[14] Show me a church that's not beleaguered in some way, and I'll show you a church that's not really in mission. Show me a leader with whom everyone is happy and I'll show a leader who's not doing her job.

Leaders of the cross, and the assembly in which they serve, we might say after the late theologian Alan Lewis, live out their existence in the grave on Holy Saturday.[15] In God's struggle with the world, the flesh, and the devil, the tide of war has turned, and the eventual victory is assured. But there are many battles yet to fight, many casualties yet to suffer, and many "brutal facts" yet to confront before, as St. Paul promises, "God is all in all" (1 Cor. 15:28). Until that day, our cross-shaped prayers and leadership are bolstered by knowing God "under the form of the opposite" and by always "saying what a thing actually is."

The Parish Proving Ground in Transition: In Sickness and in Health

The importance of facing up to the "brutal facts" of our life together is heightened when the assembly is in leadership transition. The added anxiety of being "harassed and helpless, like sheep without a shepherd" (Matt. 9:36) raises the stakes when we contemplate change. Part of the folk wisdom of congregational life is that when you are new to a ministry setting, you should not change so much as a light fixture for at least the first five years. Our mentors used to advise us to confine ourselves to trust-building activities during the early years of a fragile relationship with a community.

In practice this meant focusing your time, energy, and schedule on preaching and worship leadership, visitation of the sick and shut-ins and key people, public teaching, some semblance of organizing and administration, and so forth. As discussed in chapter 1, doing these things used to be called "paying the rent." Prove reliable in these core functions, the theory went, and you will be granted a great deal of latitude in other areas of your choice and vision.

We mentioned how this traditional counsel has come under attack in recent years. When taken to an extreme, goes the critique, "paying the rent" reduces parish practice to a narrow chaplaincy. Vision and mission take a backseat. What the critique often ignores, as we've said, is that relationship building cannot be ignored; an assembly of real people will trust the vision only if they first trust the visionary. On the other hand, the critique is correct that in practice—on the ground—the mission won't necessarily wait for you if you put it on hold while waiting for everyone to get cozy with one another!

These practical issues about trust building and change are magnified in periods of transition, especially in the aftermath of some trauma to the body of Christ. Timing now becomes even more crucial than in more "normal" circumstances. A host of questions, questions that are all of a piece, now rush to the fore and beg to be dealt with in the rough-and-tumble of decision making. How long does "recovery" go on? A couple of years? A generation? How can we measure the risks of even the smallest changes in parish life and its ministries? How should leaders in the trenches function and still be leaders?

After a while, what we learn is that we must be simultaneously firm and flexible. A good analogy is the ancient wisdom tradition that describes the good leader as a reed bending with the wind rather than a hardwood tree that snaps under stress. Thus, on the one hand, the counsel to put things on hold ("don't even change a light fixture") still has merit. On the other hand, even if our primary concern in the early years is for healing and recovery, sometimes a change in parish programming becomes a vital part of the healing and trust-building process itself. So leaders are left with the everyday dilemma that while we might not be ready for the mission, the mission won't necessarily wait for us. There are no hard-and-fast rules, nor is there a procedure manual that lists all the do's and don'ts, the various shifts of gear that may be required.

Take this case study from parish practice. Within Pastor Kim's first two years at Hope Church, three new ministry programs were under consideration: a complete revamping of the catechetical program, a new stewardship approach using an outside company, and the expansion of the worship schedule to experiment with so-called contemporary worship.

Each group had its own task force, and each kept in touch with the others. As the new senior pastor sat in the "hot seat" of interaction with these groups, they naturally wanted her input and endorsement. What she began to realize was that her real job was more like the driver-education teacher who sits on the passenger side of the vehicle but has her own brakes and steering wheel in case the car is headed into the ditch. When a group would eagerly say that it wanted to move ahead with its proposed plans, she might slip in a reminder that she was new to the congregation and ask, "Can you prove to me that the congregation is ready for this?" So a key part of leadership is frequently asking the readiness question—regarding logistical and resource readiness, group-consensus readiness, and the depth question of emotional and spiritual readiness.

In the case of the new stewardship program, which would cost some twelve thousand dollars, Pastor Kim asked, "How will it look for the new pastor to push for 'outsourcing' stewardship to a professional company? Would people think, *Who does she think she is, especially with what we've just been through?*" In the end, the task force decided to wait two years before buying into this program. As for the revamped catechetical program, the group proceeded right away. The members concluded that the existing program was in such bad shape that there was nothing to lose, and that the new program might give a small boost in morale to everyone concerned. They took a middle-ground position on changing the public worship schedule, moving ahead after spending some months fine-tuning the planning details and talking candidly with the congregation.

In other words, leadership amid change and trauma, to say nothing of "normal" circumstances, is a theological art (see chapter 4 on the "Theologian in Residence"), not an exact science. We possess a bit of received wisdom, a focus on patiently building partnerships and *constantly asking questions*. To ask questions that arise from "saying what a thing actually is" is to summon forth the faith that is within the assembly to become a faith active in works of love.

Leaders should never take the question of readiness for change upon themselves alone, but only in active partnership with the assembly as a whole, with other professional colleagues in ministry, and in the consoling knowledge of the forgiveness of sins (including the sins of the leaders!) that they hear declared from "the mutual conversation and consolation of the brothers and the sisters."[16]

Living a Double Life: The "Group Animal at War"

To all appearances, the foregoing discussion is simply about timing in our action plans. The cross-shaped leader, however, learns that the question of readiness leads to something deeper within the life of the group. The ambiguous push-pull of leadership tells us that there are realities beneath the appearances. The mature leader develops a sixth sense for "the unknown," the irrational, within the public life of the assembly.

What leader has not had the eerie intuition that something un-spoken, yet utterly real, is present within the group? The first clue may be the feeling that he has been deceived, that the group resists his efforts to carry out the publicly agreed-upon vision, mission statement, action plan, and job description. He begins to wonder: *Why are they making me crazy? Didn't we have an agreement when I was hired? I'm just doing what they asked me. Why are things so weird around here?* Welcome to the ecclesiastical Twilight Zone.

Here's what happens. The new leader shows up at Good Shepherd Church and earnestly carries out his duties in accordance with the mission statement and job description he's been given and has re-ceived in good faith. He brings in new members, revamps the cat-echetical program, and broadens the volunteer base in support of several key ministry areas. He is effective at "equipping the saints" (Eph. 4:12) through a willingness to delegate responsibilities.

All goes swimmingly until there are whispers in the parking lot (the Spanish Inquisition of parish life) that not everyone is happy with this progress in congregational life. The pastor grows to feel that within the group there's some unspoken expectation. A silent contract seems to be in effect. It's the invisible eight-hundred-pound gorilla in the room.

By praying, listening, questioning, soliciting the perspective of mentors, and standing fast, the pastor learns that in this case what the group wants, but can't voice, is *to be taken care of.* Its mem-bers not only expect the leader to "take care of them," but they also unconsciously believe that their end of the covenant bond consists primarily in "being taken care of." Because of this deep-seated anxiety over being uncared for, the publicly stated mission is either put on hold or complied with grudgingly. Dependency is the competing driving force in community life, the "pull" running counter to the "push" of the mission statement.

This dependency is often cloaked in the religious vocabulary of compassion and caregiving, which, because these are authentic bib-lical and pastoral values (hence the power of the "good shepherd" image and Jesus's command to "feed my sheep"), mask what's also going on: regressed behavior that stems from the childish fear of being abandoned. The gospel speaks of the crowds being "harassed and helpless, like sheep without a shepherd" (Matt. 9:36). The fear is utterly real and not to be disparaged.

The British Army psychiatrist Wilfred Bion was the visionary (oops!) researcher who probed and mapped the unconscious life of groups. His legacy is the field of Group Relations theory and practice. Working in group-therapy settings with officers at military hospitals toward the end of World War II, Bion began to notice that each group, no matter the composition, shifts back and forth between two levels or modes of mental functioning. One level or mode is the stated mission, task, or work that the group is supposedly organized to perform. He calls this the "Work Group." The other level or mode of functioning is always just below the surface of the group's conscious life. He calls this the "Basic Assumption Group." This theory means that even though the group is supposedly gathered to perform a stated task (selling hamburgers, making widgets, or spreading the gospel), the members are also gathered "as if" for another unspoken reason. (Note: By "group," Bion didn't mean a faction, clique, or subgroup within the group, but a mental and emotional mode within group life. Think of the "group" as having AM and FM radio modes.) The Basic Assumption Group resists and may undermine the Work Group in a kind of subconscious tug-of-war. In colorful words, Bion goes so far as to define even the individual as "a group animal at war."[17]

Bion saw a threefold pattern in "Basic Assumption" group functioning. *One,* the group gathers "as if" its main business were for the group to be taken care of. The unspoken mission is *dependency.* *Two,* the group gathers "as if" its business were to fight an unseen enemy from either within or without. The unspoken mission is *fight/flight.* And *three,* the group gathers for *pairing,* a kind of utopian dream that two people (or parties) within the group, no matter the gender, will pair off, mate, and give the promise of an unborn messiah who will lead the people into an ideal future.

Dependency is probably the most familiar "as if" to those of us in parish practice. The fight/flight "as if" is more akin to closed groups that seek an internal or external scapegoat for their problems. Churches are no stranger to this Basic Assumption, either. Pairing reminds me of the wish-dream of finding some Moses in the bulrushes of our community life (hiring the ideal new staff member, or getting the "right kind of families" to join the church) who will lead us to the Promised Land. (To maintain the pairing illusion, however, the messiah must remain unborn.) Bion observed that groups may shift back and forth between Basic Assumptions.

What the leader must awaken to is the certainty that the group will project its Basic Assumption mode onto him as a "group deity" and that in all probability, no matter how he conducts himself, he will disappoint the group expectation. The inexperienced leader may become the next victim of the group cycle of projected hope, disappointment, and replacement.

So what is this "doomed" leader to do? First, awareness that you're doomed is everything! It's the first step in breaking the Basic Assumption cycle, or rewriting the unspoken contract, or if need be, eventually "getting out of Dodge." Second, the leader must be dedicated to reality in all its unlovely guises. The cross-shaped leader does not belittle the "as if" of the community's group life, but names it and brings it to light for everyone, including himself, to view.

A note of caution: don't give in to the temptation to focus exclusively on all the gory details of Basic Assumption life within a group. This may be fun and can be like watching a group train wreck. But such psychic gawking can divert attention from the developmental thrust that is also at work to move the group forward in its mission. Bion was adamant that the Work Group is highly resilient and works its way into the group's unconscious life, too.[18] Thus, even though the Basic Assumption life of the group often resists its stated mission, the impetus to perform its task (the Work Group) can be just as powerful. The cross-shaped leader lives and works in this promise and blessed assurance. As Paul discovered in ministry, God's "power is made perfect in weakness" (2 Cor. 12:9a).

Bion arrived at his insights when he met with a group but deliberately refused to "lead" them in the sense of overtly taking over the direction of the group session in its proceedings. For the group, this approach could be maddening ("What we need here is a *real* leader!" "After all, *you're* supposed to be the expert; what are you being paid for?"), but it often brought to the fore the "Basic Assumption" that was a countervailing force within group life.

In practical terms, then, the push-pull of group life calls for the leader's use of both "directive" and "nondirective" modes of functioning. Being relentlessly directive is not proof of decisive, visionary leadership, but of plain old impatience, fussiness, and neurotic mistrust that infantilize otherwise responsible people. Good judgment about when to be directive and when not to be directive in leadership comes only with hard experience.

Each of us is a "group animal at war." The group is in us as assuredly as we are in the group. And thus the subconscious tug-of-war that is within the group lives within us as well. However, our life together need not be a grim and never-ending struggle, like that of Sisyphus rolling the rock up the hill only to have it roll back down. There are times—blessed times like the calm at the center of the storm or the clearing in the darkness of the forest—when the tug-of-war becomes a lively dance. Partners learn to do the different dance steps. And we learn that being decisive has more than one gear!

Love and Discipline: The Office of the Keys

What do we do when the Basic Assumption Group threatens to paralyze, overwhelm, and even destroy the life of the assembly? Every so often leaders find themselves put in the position of having to administer some form of community discipline. People disrupt congregational life. Although this acting out is probably some kind of cry for help, there may come a time when being "pastoral" means being an advocate for the congregation as a whole. For the sake of the community and the troubled people themselves, you may be called on to exercise a facet of one of the most neglected of the marks of the church—the Office of the Keys, the teaching authority Jesus entrusts to the community to "bind and loose" sins. Based on Matthew 16, the office has the responsibility to declare the good news that for Christ's sake God forgives our sins and makes us whole again. The word "office" emphasizes the seriousness of the matter: that God wills and intends that this be done as a direct expression of the gospel; that we trustingly receive the declaration as if from Christ himself; that repentant people might be restored to the faith community; and that the community itself might thereby be renewed. The exercise of some community discipline is an essential part of the Office of the Keys.

In these circumstances, your whole being cries out that, as a Christian, you must be caring and understanding. Yet you may reach the point at which, just as in a family or a household, authentic love is authentic only when it includes some restraint and admonition or correction. Being loving doesn't mean allowing someone to undermine the mission of the gospel or to harm other people who may not be able to defend themselves.

Do you "enjoy" these occasions? If you did, that enjoyment would be pretty sick. Even when some discipline or correction is carried out with prayer and utmost care and concern, there's no escaping the feeling that somehow you've been acting as a kind of executioner. Your apprehension that you might well be wrong, and that you are accountable before God, makes you yearn for the day of retirement. In such a circumstance, I've been known to come home and say to my spouse, "I feel dirty. This is not who I am."

Every church constitution has a section on the discipline of members, but I don't know anybody who sits up at night reading it in lieu of the jokes in *Reader's Digest*. Typically, the constitution stipulates a sequence of steps to be taken when admonishing and correcting a member. The model is always from Matthew 18: first, go to the offending party in private; second, take one or two witnesses to meet with the member; third, take the matter before the "church," which may be the board or another representative body; finally, censure or remove the person from membership. The constitution always includes cautions, appeals, and a mandate for ongoing care. Articles on discipline make for daunting reading. You realize that such a process can never be ventured on your own. If you don't have a group of strong, loving, and wise leaders with whom to administer discipline, don't even think about this undertaking. It's not something to be carried out by priestly cowboys or bounty hunters.

One of the financial officers in a congregation had the deplorable habit of verbally attacking people during public meetings.

The attacks weren't only about policy matters; they sometimes became personal. He once commented on a fellow council member's weight during a meeting. Also, it wasn't uncommon for him to write an insult on a bill he was paying if he didn't like the bookkeeping procedures of the vendor. More than once the church had to call a local business and offer its apologies. Like a Jekyll and Hyde, the man could be charming one minute and turn on people the next. He may have been what's called a "borderline personality."

Thank God for some strong and wise leaders who policed this situation without saying to the pastor, "*You're* the pastor. What are *you* going to do about it?" One night before a regular council meeting, they took the officer aside as he entered the building and asked him to sit between them during the meeting. Here's what they said to him: "Monty, when you go into the conference room, you will sit between us [a male and a female], and if there are any problems, we will squeeze your knee under the table, and you *will* be quiet." He resigned not long afterward, dropping off the books late one night when no one was in the building. All subsequent attempts to reach him with follow-up care were unsuccessful.

The Hertzogs, a middle-aged couple, had begun to hold secret meetings in their home with selectively invited members, ostensibly because they wanted to bring about some changes in parish youth programming. Because they mistrusted the staff and elected leaders, they thought it was OK to gather some presumably interested parties to lobby for change. But they worked on two fronts at once, asking for time at committee meetings to present their concerns and proposals at the same time they were holding secret meetings.

Soon it became apparent that they were also dealing with a troubling family issue at home. The local congregation had become the convenient object on which to "displace" their family distress. *If only the church would change*, their behavior seemed not so subtly to say, *everything would right itself at home.*

In a sequence of private conversations, leaders asked to meet with the couple and expressed concern that their behavior had become disruptive of the congregation. The Hertzogs denied any covert intentions and continued to insist that youth programming was the real issue. Matters came to a head when the Hertzogs' behavior adversely affected a youth outside their family. In response, the leaders firmly indicated that the couple had now made themselves the issue, rather than the pros and cons of the ministry debate. Thereafter, the leaders requested that the couple refrain from all covert activities and limit themselves to participation in worship for a period of time. After sending some angry printed communications, the Hertzogs left the congregation. Follow-up care was offered, but it was received politely and coolly.

Both during and after such episodes, you do a lot of second-guessing and have plenty of guilt feelings. You know that you might be wrong, or fear that you have overreacted. Our training, and often our temperament, is about the "care of souls." Violating this sacred trust is a nightmarish possibility for your pastoral soul. Yet exercising the Office of the Keys in the absence of any community discipline or order is no more loving or compassionate than family members' not caring enough for one another to have mutual expectations. Discipline without love is abuse; but love without discipline is neglect.

What *is* consoling is that the church is an object of faith as a living body, an assembly of people called together by the Holy Spirit. Henri Nouwen liked to remind his readers that we are called to believe in the church with the same faith with which we believe in God.[19] The ancient ecumenical creeds summarize Scripture (Matt. 16): "We believe in one holy catholic and apostolic church" (Nicene Creed); "I believe in the Holy Spirit, the holy catholic church, the communion of saints" (Apostles' Creed).

Only when the church ceases being for us a "thing" or an "it" and becomes a living assembly of people called out by the Spirit, the body of Jesus in the world, do we undertake its ministry with due humility, love, and steadfastness. This teaching that the church is a living body is consoling because we trust that the church is worth all the fuss of our efforts, even the fuss of having to exercise discipline for the sake of love. It's Christ's body, not ours. God intends the church. For all its sin and apostasy, the faith community is God-willed in its existence and mission.

True, in our moments of disillusionment, we may echo the notorious saying of the modernist French Bible scholar Alfred Loisy

(1857–1940): *"Jesus annoncait le Royaume et c'est l'Eglise qui est venue"* ("Jesus proclaimed the Kingdom, but it was the Church that came"). When we recover our biblical and theological bearings, however, we hear the voice of Jesus promise the church: "the gates of Hades will not prevail against it" (Matt. 16:18).

Ministry as Office and Person: Boundaries and Such

The Office of the Keys is a cross-shaped function for the sake of gospel wholeness and the well-being of the body and its members, but another mark of the church also has an impact on both leaders and the assembly: the Office of Ministry. By this we simply mean the public commissioning of ministers and leaders for the sake of good order and to ensure that the gospel is proclaimed. My own experience is that knowing I'm the occupant of an office is a hedge against taking personally everything that happens in parish life.

When the new pastor came to Redeemer Church many years ago, a young person used to come forward during communion each Sunday to receive the blessing. She had yet to take her first communion instruction. Early on, the pastor learned that she had been sexually abused by a family member who was no longer in the home.

How was he to touch her on the head, or anywhere else for that matter, look her in the eyes, and pronounce a blessing? Touch itself of any kind was neither safe nor welcome, or so he feared (without asking her how she felt). Conflicted, he finally spoke to her grandmother, who often brought her to church, and also conferred with a fellow pastor whose judgment he trusted. Here's what they agreed: it wasn't an option *not* to administer a touch and blessing of some kind, for that would just single her out. But neither was it an option to use eye contact, touch, and words in some highly intimate or overfamiliar manner.

Could he find safe touch and words of blessing that communicated personally yet appropriately? In practice, it meant he used a fairly reserved touch and speech that was neither impersonal nor too intimate. Somehow the family and the church staff bridged the way gracefully to her days of first communion instruction. What a relief when their human interaction was finally mediated by bread and wine and Jesus's own words rather than by ambiguous human words and touch.

This is a microcosm in which to view cross-shaped leadership as a whole. How can ministry remain personal without drawing undue attention to the leader? How can the doer disappear into the deed like service at a half-decent restaurant? How can we make what Luther calls "the doings of the saints" deeply human yet not about us? Not far from our home there's a street sign for a large independent church that reads, "Victorious Living Church: *People Matter to God.*" I always find myself talking to the car windshield and musing, *Yes, good marketing, but does God matter to the people?* Ministry, and indeed the Christian life, is not a matter of answering this question, but it is a matter of living it. *Does God matter to people?* That question suggests the difference between a disciple and a consumer or customer. The consumer wants satisfaction; the disciple wants the Word. The customer is always right; the disciple is always forgiven in order to serve.

One of the untapped resources leaders have to ensure that ministry is not about us, but it is still personal, is the Office of Ministry. My task is not to give a historical account of this concept. What's crucial is that in the daily life of parish practice, leaders are able to distinguish between the office and the person of ministry. Hear the good news: we are not our work, nor are we our rank and office. It's one thing for us to say this; it's another thing for it to become part of the fiber of our being. Yet the more seriously we take this theological distinction to heart, the more likely it is that we will be able to be in mission without personalizing (taking personally) every joy and sorrow, every success and failure.

Let me illustrate with a reminiscence that Henri Nouwen once shared with me over dinner. Father Henri said that when he was in the seminary in the Netherlands, and then when he was first ordained as a priest, he and his fellow students and priests never did anything without wearing their clerical collars. It got to the point, he said, "where we practically did chin-ups on our collars when we went to sleep at night. They were grafted into the skin of our necks."

When he first came to America and began his teaching career at the University of Notre Dame, it was the same. One day some friends invited him to the Indianapolis Motor Speedway, but he said he didn't want to go because he knew that if he went dressed like a priest, something would happen and he'd be called on to help. His friends prevailed, and he went. "Sure enough," Father Henri said, "there was a crash, and I was asked to come to the scene." I'm not sure I ever saw Father Henri with a clerical collar—either at dinner that night or thereafter.

While "uniforms" and other trappings of office may do more harm than good (or not!), the office itself and a public commissioning thereto are meant to give some assurance that the gospel is not completely at the mercy of its human messengers. Moreover, to trust that one has been called to an office and not to a position of either personal privilege or burdensome responsibility brings great relief. We are freed and empowered to use our gifts without either paralyzing fear or overweening pride. Yet the office contains a call to duty that demands our every human talent and strength.

The wider context of the Office of Ministry is Christian vocation and the gospel of salvation by God's grace alone. In the teaching of my faith tradition, which happens to be Lutheran, we like to say, after Martin Luther himself, that God doesn't need our good works. Our neighbor does, though. So it is with our vocation or calling. God doesn't need my vocation, whether in daily life or as a public office.[20] Certainly, God doesn't need a pastor! Or a minister of any sort. God's doing just fine, thank you. In heaven things are running smoothly. What cries for help are things on earth.

Thus, the people around us need our vocations—and can and often do benefit from them as we carry them out in daily life as well as in the public offices of ministry: The guy across the street or across the office. The woman around the block. The kid next door. The people down at church, the assembly of believers and would-be believers. And neighbors both near and far. They all need our vocations. So the bad news is that God doesn't need my ministry at all. But that's also the good news, for now we need not play God in ministry, expecting glory or fearing shame for our triumphs and failures. Repeat after me: "I am *not* my work; I am *not* my rank and office."

Moreover, even here—that is, on earth—we are in no way responsible for anyone's conversion or spiritual growth. The gospel itself, and it alone, works such grace. As theologian Robert Kolb says, "Only the gospel itself can guarantee the gospel."[21] Ministers merely apply the gospel. What the gospel does and what the human messenger does are as far apart as heaven and earth. (See chapter 1 on "passive" and "active" righteousness.) Failure to live this gracious distinction between heaven and earth is the source of every cult. And it makes one crazy, too. Remember: it's the incarnation (in contemporary theological parlance, Jesus as "God with skin on"), and not my ministry (whether on Sunday *or* Monday), that bridges the chasm between heaven and earth.

In the end, we may not exactly be "exalted" when we imagine we will, but the promise is that we shall certainly begin to find some order in "the fine mess" of our allotted ministry.

Summary

1. Cross-shaped leaders are those who look at the "brutal facts" of our life together and do not turn away in revulsion. They trust that God is at work *sub contrario specie*, "under the form of the opposite," and therefore they develop the professional skills to "call the thing what it actually is." They look for God amid God's "unattractive" works.

2. The "marks of the church" give life to the assembly; they originate the assembly. The various clinical and managerial models of renewal are adjuncts and tools whose theological underpinning is the assembly as a function of its marks.

3. The Christian assembly, like all human groups, is driven by a subconscious tug-of-war between its publicly stated mission and primitive anxieties to be taken care of, to fight or flee from an unseen enemy, and to await the "better days ahead" that an unborn savior will bring.

4. The Office of the Keys is responsible for declaring the forgiveness of sins for Christ's sake. It is also a steward of community discipline in the form of admonition and correction.

5. The Office of Ministry is for the sake of good order and the continuity over time of the assembly's proclamation and varied ministries. It is the public face of Christian, baptismal vocation and the ministry of the whole people of God.

❖ Questions for Discussion

1. Read about Paul's struggle with the Jerusalem "mother church" (Gal. 1 and 2; Acts 15) over which agenda for mission (to the Jews or to the Gentiles) would take precedence. What compromise did the parties reach? How did they reach their accord?

2. On a scale of one to ten with ten being the highest, what is your degree of dedication to looking squarely at the "brutal facts" of your ministry setting? Do you tend to avoid confrontation, and to what degree? Why?

3. What are the Work Group (the stated mission) and the Basic Assumption Group (dependency, fight/flight, or pairing) in your current ministry setting? Are you able to accept the Basic Assumption for what it is, yet patiently go about the task of possibly rewriting the group's subconscious covenant?

4. Think of a time when you, together with others, had to administer some discipline for the sake of the well-being of the body of Christ. How would you do it differently the next time?

5. How can the Office of Ministry that you occupy help you not take things personally? Or is the office more of an unbearable weight? When is it one, and when is it the other?

HUMOR
The Last Laugh

Sour looks and plain garments do not a Christian make! —Martin Luther[1]

Humor . . . is emotional chaos remembered in tranquility. —James Thurber[2]

If only we'd stop trying to be happy, we'd have a pretty good time.
—Edith Wharton[3]

What is laughter? What is laughter?
It is God waking up! O it is God waking up!
It is the sun poking its sweet head out
From behind a cloud
You have been carrying too long,
Veiling your eyes and heart . . .
It is the glorious sound
Of a soul waking up! —Hafiz[4]

That beloved grouch Mark Twain, who had a love-hate relationship with his Presbyterian upbringing, at least had the genius to see that the true dignity of humankind is its gift for laughter:

For your race, in its poverty, has unquestionably one really effective weapon—laughter. Power, money, persuasion, supplication, persecution—these can lift a colossal humbug—push it a little—weaken it a little, century by century; but only laughter can blow it to rags and atoms at a blast. Against the assault of laughter nothing stands.[5]

This final chapter means to pay homage not only to Twain but also to all those saintly souls for whom "the whole armor of God" (Eph. 6) includes the sword of godly, and therefore good, humor. For the colossal humbug that is in all of us must die the gentle death of a thousand laughs. Levity is the opposite of gravity and heaviness. It's the soul's taking itself lightly, and therefore it reveals our urgent need for grace.

So in response to those jaded souls who think that church work is dull and lifeless, I offer the following documentary evidence that ministry has its madcap moments and that it may even be a contact sport. Consider this 2003 article from *The Philadelphia Inquirer:*

Pastor faces charges
Lebanon (AP)—An arrest warrant has been issued for a Serbian Orthodox church pastor who allegedly threatened to shoot the church's new council president during a dispute over church policy, but ended up getting shot in the foot himself.

For more of the gory details about the parish dispute that led to the confrontation, simply Google a few keywords. The results include even the description of a wrestling match between the two protagonists as they made their way around church property before the climactic moment when the pastor pulled out his 9mm semiautomatic pistol. Talk about "equipping the saints"! You'll be glad for your present more-or-less nonviolent ministry.

Or consider the following church activity notice in a weekend edition of the Allentown, Pennsylvania, *Morning Call* from the mid-1980s:

Revival meeting
There will be a revival meeting this Sunday afternoon at 3:00 PM at ———— Methodist Church, R.D. #10, Allentown. Johnny Berguson and his horse Sheik will appear. Sheik will perform tricks—Berguson will share biblical principles.

What you need to know is that the traveling evangelist lost his beloved horse just a few years ago. He (the horse) died peacefully of old age at the Cornell University veterinary hospital. Sheik, whose full name was Al-Marah Majestic Sheik, was of obvious Arabian lineage. Thus, Johnny and Sheik were an ecumenical duo. Sheik lives on as the patron saint of the company (check out the website) that his owner now operates in central Pennsylvania, a company that sells recording products for churches. I am not making this up.

You Can't Make This Stuff Up

The theologian Reinhold Niebuhr says in his oft-cited 1949 essay on humor and faith that laughter should cease when we enter the sanctuary itself, but I'm not so sure.[6] Thus, I thought twice about including here Martin Luther's report in *Table Talk,* "About a Dog Who Was Lutheran." If ever there was a passage that might be said to border on "potty mouth," it would be this one:

> The doctor [Martin Luther] said, "I just received a letter from Jonas [Justus]. He wrote that a dog had shit into the grave of the bishop of Halle. I believe it's fatal, for it has also happened to others before. Once when there was a procession with banners around a church, the verger [the procession leader] put the holy water pot on the ground. A dog came along and pissed into the holy water pot. A priest noticed this because he was sprinkling the water, and he said, 'You impious dog! Have you become a Lutheran too?'"[7]

I have it on good authority (note to editor: never mind who, OK?) that this sixteenth-century dog is an ancestor whose direct descendant may be the poodle who sat on a beetle during church in Mark Twain's *The Adventures of Tom Sawyer:*

> Then there was a wild yelp of agony and the poodle went sailing up the aisle; the yelps continued, and so did the dog; he crossed the house in front of the altar; he flew down the other aisle; he crossed before the doors; he clamored up the home-stretch; his anguish grew with his progress, till presently he was but a wooly comet moving in its orbit with

the gleam and the speed of light. At last the frantic sufferer sheered from its course, and sprang in to its master's lap; he flung it out of the window, and the voice of distress quickly thinned away and died in the distance.[8]

Here is proof, if there need be, that the sins of the parents, albeit canine, visit themselves upon the children well beyond the third and fourth generations of which the Hebrew Scriptures warn. With apologies to Professor Niebuhr, then, it seems that even in the holy of holies we professional religionists may at times be exposed like the Wizard of Oz. When Toto pulls back the curtain, and our sacramental dials and levers are bared, we cry out, "Pay no attention to that man behind the curtain!" Our pretensions may follow us all the way to the altar of living sacrifice.

Church workers often share such reminiscences and perhaps keep a file with items like the foregoing. Our church follies warn us about what often happens when we seek some glory other than the cross. But these follies may also be consoling, for they free us from the overbearing weight of taking ourselves so seriously.

Humor: "A Big Bracket Around the Seriousness of the Present"

In his *Church Dogmatics,* the Swiss theologian Karl Barth placed his brief discussion of humor at the very end of Part III, the Doctrine of Creation. The God of Hebrews and Christians breathed the world into existence (Gen. 1), but for many ancient peoples this same breath was also said to be "risible," that is, the breath that enlivens our laughter. Thus, for some of Israel's neighbors, especially the Egyptians, God *laughs* the world into existence. The breath of life literally bellows, "Ha, ha, ha." Compared to this creative laugh, scholar Barry Sanders notes, "the envious hiss of the serpent sounds like an old tire giving up its air."[9]

For Barth, humor is an acknowledgment of humankind's creaturely "freedom in limitation."[10] The improbable reality that in Jesus Christ eternity does indeed crisscross with time, that "God is with us" in a manger, on a cross, and in the grave, is so astonishing that the resulting folly of God's wisdom can be witnessed to only by humor. St. Paul might proclaim this unlikely divine presence as "the foolishness of the cross" (1 Cor. 1:18).

Here creaturely limitation is no shame at all but a real honor. That we are limited beings is not our disgrace but precisely our glory. And our limitation honors God, too, because until Christ returns in glory, we are fully human only when we are *co*-human with God and with one another. True humanity is co-humanity, and it is the basis of all ethical action.[11] Martin Luther liked to put this covenant in terms of the Great Commandment—the love of God above all and of the neighbor as yourself.

In an earlier work *Ethics* (1928–1929) Barth defines humor as "a big bracket around the seriousness of the present." Humor is fitting to our dignity as children of God. Children, it is said, laugh on average some three hundred times a day. Adults laugh only seventeen times a day. Serious researchers say that this statistic is not at all true, and that in fact adults may laugh much more. The more we're together—be we young or old, shy or gregarious—the more we may laugh; the more we're alone (Greta Garbo's plea, "I vant to be alone," comes to mind), the more strait-laced we may be. The variable is social interaction, not age. As "children" of God who look to God for our very existence and for all good things, Barth insists, we cannot take ourselves with "ultimate seriousness." To do so usurps God's place as God. If we take grace seriously, we cannot take ourselves with a seriousness that is finality. Barth writes:

> Humor means the placing of a big bracket around the seriousness of the present. In no way does it mean—and those who think it does do not know what real humor is—that this seriousness is set aside or dismissed. Humor arises, and can only arise, when we wrestle with this seriousness of the present. But above and in this wrestling, we cannot be totally serious as the children of God.[12]

Yes, there are many things that are serious in this life, things that we dare not make light of or ridicule. But for the children of God such seriousness cannot be the last word. Barth writes: "Like art, humor undoubtedly means that we do not take the present with ultimate seriousness, not because it is not serious enough in itself, but because God's future, which breaks into the present, is more serious."[13] Humor of a certain caste (see below) is the "last laugh" beyond any ultimate seriousness.

Barth goes on to ground humor in the experience of suffering: "Of humor, too, one may say that it is genuine when it is the child of suffering." In so doing, he appeals to Luther, for whom, Barth says, humor is befitting those who have been "assaulted . . . [and] have been through the wringer." True humor is to be sought "among those who suffer from blows such as those that smote Job."[14] When humor is grounded in *shared suffering*, Barth continues, then we have some guidance to distinguish *true humor* from *false humor*. True humor "presupposes rather than excludes the knowledge of suffering." Its favorite target is ourselves rather than others. Self-deprecating humor is different from that of the carnival. True humor "sees the bracket in which the self stands."[15]

One way laughter "brackets" the self is through cathartic release. For instance, as I was leaving the hospital bedside of a man who had some intestinal blockage that the doctors could not pinpoint,

I mistakenly said, "Maurice, I hope they get to the bottom of things." "Pastor," he said, "I think they've already been there." His generous wit overcame my pastoral ineptness. Barth continues:

> For this reason and in this way it has the significance of a liberation and release rather than poison and gall. . . . When we have first laughed at ourselves we can laugh at others, and we can stand cheerfully the final test of being laughed at by them—a test which many supposedly humorous people ignominiously fail. The seriousness of real joy applies here no less than in art. The total seriousness of decision in face of God's command can reach a climax in our having to laugh and not just cry and gnash our teeth, in our having to make the best of a bad job.[16]

Such a comedown reminds me of a recent Sunday service at which a man collapsed during the final hymn. Fortunately, we had in attendance three nurses, a physician's assistant, and a retired dentist, all of whom came to his aid. When I arrived on the scene just as he was regaining consciousness, he looked up and said, "Oh no, you're the last person I want to see." Then the paramedics arrived.

Apropos of "the bracket in which the self stands," I can only hope that Barth would have enjoyed (he died in 1968, so this is a possibility only within the communion of saints) the snapshot of a young seminary intern riding a donkey in a gymnasium during what is termed a "donkey basketball game." The senior pastor thought it would be good public relations for the staff to participate in this community fund-raising event. You say you don't know what donkey basketball is? Don't ask. Believe me, it's no Palm Sunday procession. Perhaps it's because my hometown of Clinton, Iowa, is the birthplace (he's buried there, too) of Felix Adler, the first "King of Clowns" from the original Barnum and Bailey Circus, that I, the helmeted vicar spotted riding on an ass, feel a certain kinship with the religious tradition of what is called "the holy fool."

The medieval "Feast of the Ass" is the obvious paradigm here. As satirized by the Enlightenment philosopher Voltaire, legend has it that the donkey that carried Jesus into Jerusalem on Palm Sunday later made its way across the Mediterranean and settled in Verona,

Italy, where its remains were kept in an artificial ass made for the purpose by forty monks of Our Lady of the Organs. Carried in procession twice a year, the ass was honored with a magnificent funeral. Soon the feast spread to other countries and was particularly popular in France (the donkey metamorphosed into the one the Holy Family used to escape into Egypt), where during mass the ass's praise was sung: "From the Eastern lands the Ass is come, beautiful and very brave, well fitted to bear burdens. Up! Sir Ass, and sing. Open your pretty mouth. Hay will be yours in plenty, and oats in abundance." At the end of the mass, the priest, in lieu of saying, "Go, this is the dismissal," is instructed to bray three times; and the people, instead of responding "Thanks be to God," say "Hinham, hinham, hinham."[17]

Puncturing the Balloon of the False Self and the Closet Atheist

Laughter is a critic of authority and "the establishment." Laughter is prophetic, as when Nathan confronts David and reminds the king that he has been found out (2 Sam. 12:7). Laughter stands in the town square and announces that the emperor wears no clothes. It says, "You can't fool all of the people all of the time." As chronicled wonderfully by Barry Sanders, the history of laughter is in large part a history of social dissent.

The inspired lunacy of satirists—from Aristophanes to Chaucer ("The Miller's Tale" from *The Canterbury Tales*) to Voltaire to Mark Twain (*The Adventures of Huckleberry Finn*, chapter 20, on the Pokeville camp meeting) to Charlie Chaplin to the Marx Brothers to Monty Python ("The Spanish Inquisition," "The Silly Vicar," the prep-school chapel scene from *The Meaning of Life*) to the Church Lady of *Saturday Night Live*—has always served a happily subversive social agenda.

Though he banned the movie in Germany, Adolf Hitler obtained for himself a copy of Chaplin's *The Great Dictator* (1940), with its darkly satirical portrayal of Adenoid Hynkel, dictator of Tomania. Hitler is said to have watched the film twice. In the antiwar comic masterpiece *Duck Soup* (1933), Groucho Marx plays Rufus T. Firefly, the newly appointed leader of Fredonia. In response to the lavish welcome ceremony hosted by Mrs. Teasdale (Margaret Dumont), Firefly sings, "If you think this country's bad off now, just wait 'til I get through with it!" And in his last one-man show at Carnegie Hall in 1972, an aging Groucho related this incident from a visit to Montreal, Quebec, years before. As Groucho was making a quick exit from an elevator, a priest walked up to him, put out his hand, and said, "I wanna thank you for all the joy you've put into this world." Groucho shook the priest's hand, and said, "And I wanna thank you for all the joy you've taken out of this world." The priest said, "Could I use that next Sunday in my sermon?" Groucho said, "Yes you can, but you'll have to pay the William Morris office 10 percent."[18]

The lesson here is that if cleanliness is next to godliness, then seriousness is next to godlessness. People who come by their atheism honestly may still have a robust sense of humor (though foulmouthed, the late comedian George Carlin comes to mind), but have you ever known a closet atheist who could do anything but laugh nervously? Humorlessness, it seems, is the price we pay when we believe that everything depends upon us and that others can't be trusted to do what they're supposed to. And as for the false self's search for glory: is there anything it dreads more in this world than the exposure of its own foolishness?

Laughter as Law and Gospel

As godly play, humor is a theological enterprise. Laughter and humor are a healthy, indeed *prophetic*, response to the contradictions and foibles of humankind and creaturely existence. Again, Reinhold Niebuhr observes that laughter contains "a nice mixture of mercy and judgment, of censure and forbearance . . . There is judgment, therefore, in our laughter. But we also prove by laughter that we do not take the annoyance too seriously."[19] This tension reminds me of the caption for the cartoon of the forlorn preacher saying to his congregation, "I've stopped expecting you to make leaps of faith, but it would be nice to see a hop now and then."[20]

The Christian gospel has always been an "in spite of" faith. For Christ's sake, God loves us in spite of ourselves. Humor's built-in tension between judgment and mercy is, in my view, an analogy of what theologians call law and gospel. Laughter can express both the no of God's law, with its impossible demands, and the yes of the gospel, with its unconditional pardon, when the two are in unresolved tension.

Martin Luther taught us to listen for the counterpoint of God's no and God's yes in hearing the Scriptures and the proclamation of the church. Distinguishing law and gospel is a way of hearing Scripture and proclamation as either a righteous demand or an unconditional promise. When proclamation "gives us the guilts" or strikes us as a kind of spiritual "couldda, shouldda, wouldda," we are experiencing law and its righteous demands. When proclamation consoles us and smites us with a "no strings attached" pardon and promise, we are experiencing gospel.

Law and gospel aren't about different kinds of biblical literature—say, the lists of the commandments in Exodus and Deuteronomy versus the Gospel of Mark as a book. Rather, it's about what the Scripture and proclamation *do to us*. For example, the Twenty-third Psalm ("The Lord is my shepherd, I shall not want") is from the Hebrew Scriptures of our Old Testament, but when you read it, hear it, or better, sing it, it comes to you as comforting "good news." And when you hear Jesus say in the Sermon on the Mount, "You have heard that it was said, 'You shall not commit adultery.' But I say to you that everyone who looks at a woman with lust has already committed adultery" (Matt. 5:27–28), it may be written in one of the Gospels, but it strikes you as the righteous demand of the law.

One of humor's great services is to express the tangle of God's no and yes. It does so by using such elements as surprise, exaggeration, and incongruity. Even an avowed atheist like comedian George Carlin succeeds here: "God doesn't really love you, but he thinks you have a great personality."[21] At the cross there is a resolution of judgment and mercy. How so? Because only at the cross do we learn that the no is *for the sake of* the yes, that judgment is for the sake of mercy, and that the impossible demands of the law drive us into the loving and forgiving arms of Christ. We hear echoes of St. Paul: "For the Son of God, Jesus Christ, whom we proclaimed among you . . . was not 'Yes and No'; but in him it is always 'Yes.' For in him every one of God's promises is a 'Yes'" (2 Cor. 1:19–20).

If we think of humor on a spectrum from satire, which is subversive, to gentle laughter, we find ourselves moving from judgment to mercy, law to gospel. Gentle irony, some jokes, some cartoons, and some twists of language may be fluid and pliable enough to mimic the tension of no and yes, and yet to escort us to the threshold of the gospel. Ponder this: the root of the word "humor" is "fluid" or "moisture." Like humility, humor is a basic element of this earth.

This anecdote from *Reader's Digest* is a multipurpose sermon illustration that never seems to grow tired, and it celebrates our confusion over the proclamation of God's no and yes: "Overheard: My greatest fear is that I will be standing behind Mother Teresa in the Final Judgment line and I'll hear God tell her, 'You know, you should have done more.'"[22]

For me, cartoons and jokes from religious publishers rarely have much edge to them. Unlike, say, Gary Larson's sardonic *Far Side* depictions of devils, angels, and God, denominationally sponsored humor can seem sanitized. A few church-journal cartoonists, however, do seem able to illustrate the paradoxical heart of the gospel of grace.

Cartoonist Rob Portlock playfully stands astride the mystery of faith active in works . . . and of judgment and grace.

"What do you think? Should we pray or paddle?"

". . . and whatever you do, Harry, don't demand to get everything that's coming to you!"

Cartoonists Mary Chambers and Doug Hall endearingly call attention to our all-too-human condition before God and the promise of transformation:

"Well, I haven't actually *died to sin*, but I did feel kind of faint once."

"This is my fourth sermon on the transforming power of the gospel. Why do you look like the same old bunch?"

Caricaturist and religion professor James Taylor's *A Porcine History of Philosophy and Religion* became something of a cult classic upon its publication in 1972.[23] It briefly reappeared in the early 1990s. Taylor sketches pig caricatures of historical philosophers and religious denominations. Their lack of malice makes them good stress relievers for students:

LUTHERAN PIG DEALING WITH ADVERSARY

ORTHODOX PRESBYTERIAN PIG LOOKING FOR SIGNS OF GRACE REVEALED

ANGLICAN PIG FOLLOWING
THE VIA MEDIA

METHODIST PIG WHOSE HEART
HAS BEEN STRANGELY WARMED

SOUTHERN BAPTIST PIG CAUGHT UP
IN THE HEAT OF ECUMENICAL FERVOR

KIERKEGAARDIAN PIG DEMONSTRATING
A LEAP OF FAITH

The Last Laugh: Humor as Consolation

Laughter may be cutting and subversive, but it can also be consoling. In a public lecture, the Quaker spiritual writer Richard Foster once made a play on words in which he referred to the 1969 pop-psychology self-help classic, *I'm OK, You're OK*. Foster told his audience that the Christian version of the book would be this: *I'm Not OK, You're Not OK, But That's OK*.[24] The word play intimates the heart of the gospel of grace not as self-help, but as the forgiveness of sin and making people whole.

The gentle humor here is consoling because in its verbally playful way it proclaims that the reality that things are not OK is never the last word. In life and in leadership, things are indeed not OK. But that's OK! Long ago Sigmund Freud recognized how humor, as he put it, "saves on the expenditure of psychic resources."[25] Humor is the soul's safety valve, providing catharsis and displacement even in the face of death. I once heard an interview with Billy Graham and his wife, Ruth. When asked whether she had ever considered divorce, Ruth Graham wryly said, "Oh, no! Murder, maybe, but divorce, no."

As I said at the outset of this book, ministry is an impossible possibility. To say this is no ploy; it's utterly real. To characterize ministry as somehow humanly manageable is, as Churchill might say, the cruelty of false hope. Here the cross is our reality check. For the more the cross shapes our life in ministry, the more we find the working of God *sub contrario specie* ("under the form of the opposite"), and we are empowered to "say what a thing actually is."

This same cross, however, promises that the endgame (resurrection!) belongs to God and to God alone. Moreover, it promises that along the way those works of God that seem "unattractive" to us are in reality "eternal merits." Through the grave and gate of death, and through all the little graves and gates of death that litter our roads like potholes after a long winter of the soul, we find safe passage. Godly humor is the promise of a "last laugh," a compassionate laugh, beyond the scornful laughing of this world. Cross-shaped leaders are marked by the religion of good humor.[26]

Quaker theologian Howard Macy has written:

> We can laugh with rather than at. We can puncture pomposity while recognizing our own propensity to pride. We can chuckle at the foibles and failures of others, yet do so with a spirit that acknowledges them as our foibles as well. . . . Compassionate humor embraces more than it embarrasses. As we laugh arm-in-arm, we can go forward together in all our human weakness and human possibility.[27]

The spirit of such laughter is the spirit of a shared humanity with its shared suffering. Instead of the biting satire that arises from the conviction that we are, in the end, all on our own, such gentle laughter is a witness to reconciliation—reconciliation to our creaturely status and, with it, to our neighborly calling.

Martin Luther is reputed to have said, "If I'm not allowed to laugh in heaven, I do not want to go there." Amen, Brother Martin. Heaven must surely be God's last laugh on "the world, the flesh, and the devil." Yet God's last laugh must also be gentle and consoling, not the derisive or scoffing laugh of Psalm 2: "He who sits in the heavens laughs; the Lord has them in derision." God's last laugh would be like Abraham's and Sarah's laugh upon hearing of the impossible possibility of pregnancy, perhaps even Abraham's rolling around on the ground in stitches at the improbable blessing (Gen. 17; 18). God's laughter is laughter incarnate, "in the flesh," as the very name of their miracle son Isaac ("he who laughs") suggests. Most certainly it is the fulfillment of Jesus's promise: "Blessed are you who weep now, for you will laugh" (Luke 6:21).

Years ago, Jacob and Mary Svaby were two of our congregation's shut-ins. Then in their nineties, they had come to this country as immigrants from Czechoslovakia. They were devout, praying together as a couple every day by using their old Slovak prayer books. If you went to their home to bring communion, they would tell you that just before your arrival they had mutually confessed to and absolved one another, naming the things for which they were sorry in their treatment of one another that week. This was a custom they said they had carried over from the old country.

Each Christmas when the church council went caroling, Jacob and Mary's home was the last stop of the evening. Jacob was known to offer a particularly potent Slovenian plum beverage called slivovitz. Once his great nephew, who was president of the council, asked him, "Jake, are you afraid to die?" With a gentle and serene smile on his face, he wryly said to us all, "Me no afraid. Nobody come back and complain yet." This side of the grave, that's one of the few credible witnesses to the resurrection that make any gospel sense to me. And the witness came with a consoling laugh.

Leaders of the cross—who are made, not born—learn to laugh arm in arm as they go forward together with the Christian assembly in all their human weakness and human possibility. Their mutual laughter accompanies them through that daily sorrow for sin and the repentance whose promise is the gospel itself. God's last laugh, the resurrection of the dead, and of all that is dead within us as the children of Adam and Eve, must surely be the great reversal, and overcoming, of our last proud day. This is most certainly true.

Summary

1. As a part of the doctrine of creation, humor is a theological enterprise. The scriptural tradition of God's breathing the world and humankind into existence extends to laughter as the "risible" air of life, the breath behind the exclamation "ha, ha, ha!" Laughter is the "levity" that counteracts the heaviness, the "gravity," of life.

2. The history and uses of laughter in society are often subversive. Laughter is part of social dissent. Its target is often authority and "the establishment." It can be prophetic.

3. Humor is a form of catharsis. It's a safety valve for our souls. And it may express and shape our shared suffering.

4. Humor works by the use of surprise, incongruity, exaggeration, and word play.

5. Humor can express judgment and mercy simultaneously. In this way it can convey the tension between the no of law and the yes of gospel. The more that humor is consoling, the more it may lead us to the verge of the gospel itself.

❀ Questions for Discussion

1. Read the story of Abraham's and Sarah's laughter in Genesis 17 and 18. Why does Abraham fall on the ground laughing? Why does Sarah deny her laughing? What does their laughter protect them from? What's laughably impossible in your ministry and life right now?

2. Recall a time in a pastoral care setting when the use of humor arose naturally and was a consoling gift. Recall a time—perhaps at a meeting—when you may have "crossed the line" with some sarcastic remark.

3. What forms of humor do you use, and what are your favorites, in your preaching and teaching ministries?

4. Are there gender differences in our humor preferences? Is there any truth to that theory, or might it be a matter of temperament?

For instance, when it's said in watercooler conversation that women don't understand what men see in the Three Stooges, what misunderstanding does this assumption betray?

NOTES

Works frequently cited in the notes have been identified by the following abbreviations:

BC: The Book of Concord: The Confessions of the Evangelical Lutheran Church. Edited by Robert Kolb and Timothy J. Wengert. Minneapolis: Fortress, 2000.

CD: Karl Barth, *Church Dogmatics*, 4 vols., 13 parts. Edited by G. W. Bromiley and T. F. Torrance. Edinburgh: T.&T. Clark, 1936–1969.

LC: Large Catechism.

Inst. **and LCC:** John Calvin, *Institutes of the Christian Religion.* Edited by John T. McNeill and translated by Ford Lewis Battles, 2 vols., Library of Christian Classics. Philadelphia: Westminster, 1960.

LW: Luther's Works. Edited by Jaroslav Pelikan and Helmut T. Lehmann. 56 vols. Philadelphia: Fortress; St. Louis: Concordia, 1955–1986.

NRSV: New Revised Standard Version of the Holy Bible. New York: HarperCollins, 1989.

SA: Smalcald Articles.

EPIGRAPH

1. Dietrich Bonhoeffer, *Life Together*, trans. Daniel W. Bloesch and James H. Burtness (Minneapolis: Fortress, 1996), 37.

2. Ronald Rolheiser, *The Holy Longing: The Search for a Christian Spirituality* (New York: Doubleday, 1999), 128.

INTRODUCTION

1. Richard Sennett, *The Corrosion of Character* (New York: W.W. Norton, 1997), 118.

2. Richard Sennett, *The Culture of the New Capitalism* (New Haven: Yale University Press, 2006), 102.

CHAPTER 1

1. Gerhard Forde, *On Being a Theologian of the Cross: Reflections on Luther's Heidelberg Disputation, 1518* (Grand Rapids: Eerdmans, 1996), 3–4.

2. Rolheiser, *The Holy Longing*, 74.

3. Henri J. M. Nouwen, "A Spirituality of Waiting," in *The Weavings Reader,* ed. John Mogabgab (Nashville: Upper Room Books, 1993), 72.

4. *Exposition of Psalm 127, for the Christians at Riga in Livonia* (1524), in *LW* 45:330.

5. Conrad W. Weiser, *Healers: Harmed and Harmful* (Minneapolis: Fortress, 1994), 1–13.

6. Forde, *On Being a Theologian of the Cross,* 3–4.

7. Timothy J. Wengert, "'Peace, Peace . . . Cross, Cross': Reflections on How Martin Luther Relates the Theology of the Cross to Suffering," in *Theology Today* 59 (July 2002), 196.

8. *Sayings in Which Luther Found Comfort* (1530) in *LW* 41:177.

9. W. H. Vanstone, *The Stature of Waiting* (New York: Morehouse, 1982, 2006), 1–34.

10. Reinhard Hutter, *Suffering Divine Things,* trans. Doug Stott (Grand Rapids: Eerdmans, 2000), 30–31, 124–132.

11. Nouwen, "A Spirituality of Waiting," 72.

12. Martin Luther, *The 1529 Holy Week and Easter Sermons of Dr. Martin Luther,* trans. Irving L. Sandberg (St. Louis: Concordia, 1999), 67.

13. Ibid., 91.

14. Ibid.

15. Ibid.

16. C. S. Lewis, *Mere Christianity* (New York: Macmillan, 1960), 169.

17. Oswald Bayer, *Living by Faith: Justification and Sanctification,* trans. Geoffrey W. Bromiley (Grand Rapids: Eerdmans, 2003), 19–41.

18. *The Bondage of the Will* (1525) in *LW* 33:70.

19. *LW* 26:4–12; and Robert Kolb and Charles P. Arand, *The Genius of Luther's Theology: A Wittenberg Way of Thinking for the Contemporary Church* (Grand Rapids: Baker Academic, 2008), 21–52.

20. *LW* 45:331.

21. Bayer, *Living by Faith,* 36.

22. Ibid.

23. Lyle Schaller, *44 Steps Up Off the Plateau* (Nashville: Abingdon, 1993), 67–68.

24. Thom S. Rainer, "Successful leaders hold to a vision," Church Central.com (Jan. 2005), *http://www.churchcentral.com/nw/s/ template/Article.html/id/21839* (accessed May 6, 2008).

25. Howard E. Friend, "The Failure to Form Basic Partnerships: Resolving a Dilemma of New Pastorates," *Congregations* (September/October, 2002), under "The Congregation: In Depth," *http://www.pbs.org/thecongregation/indepth/resolvingdilemma.html* (accessed Dec. 7, 2007).

26. Dietrich Bonhoeffer, *Life Together,* trans. John W. Doberstein (New York: Harper & Row, 1954), 26.

27. Bayer, *Living by Faith,* 36.

28. *LW* 45:330–331.

29. *LW* 45:331.

30. Edwin Friedman, *Generation to Generation: Family Process in Church and Synagogue* (New York: Guilford Press, 1985), 208–210.

31. Parker Palmer, *The Promise of Paradox* (Washington, D.C.: Servant Leadership School, 1993), 50.

32. *SA,* 4, 45 in *BC,* 3.

CHAPTER 2

1. Thomas Merton, *New Seeds of Contemplation* (New York: New Directions, 1961), 34.

2. Palmer, *The Promise of Paradox,* 41.

3. Robert Farrar Capon, *The Foolishness of Preaching* (Grand Rapids: Eerdmans, 1998), 10.

4. Christoph Blumhardt, *Action in Waiting* (Farmington, Pa.: Bruderhof Publishing, 1998), 72.

5. Parker J. Palmer, *A Hidden Wholeness: The Journey Toward an Undivided Life* (San Francisco: Jossey-Bass, 2004), 1–49.

6. James Finley, *Merton's Palace of Nowhere* (Notre Dame, Ind.: Ave Maria Press, 2003), 73.

7. David G. Benner, *The Gift of Being Yourself* (Downers Grove, Ill.: InterVarsity Press, 2004), 79–80.

8. *The Penguin Dictionary of Epigrams,* ed. M. J. Cohen (New York: Penguin, 2001), 335.

9. *Lectures on Romans* (1515–1516), in *LW* 25:313.

10. *LC* 4, 65, in *BC,* 465.

11. *LC* 4, 66, in *BC,* 465.

12. *LC* 4, 76, in *BC,* 466.

13. *Lectures on Galatians* (1535) in *LW* 26:167.

14. Randall C. Zachman, *John Calvin as Teacher, Pastor, and Theologian* (Grand Rapids: Baker Academic, 2006), 99.

15. John Calvin, *Inst.* 1. 1. 1, in LCC 1:35.

16. Ibid.

17. *Inst.* 1. 1. 1., in LCC 1:37.

18. *Inst.* 1. 1. 2., in LCC 1:37.

19. Merton, *New Seeds of Contemplation,* 33–34.

20. Ibid., 34.

21. Ibid., 35.

22. Ibid.

23. Ibid., 38.

24. Ibid.

25. Ibid., 39.

26. Karen Horney, *Neurosis and Human Growth* (New York: W.W. Norton, 1950), 17.

27. Ibid., 18.

28. Ibid., 18–19.

29. Ibid., 19.

30. Ibid., 22.

31. Ibid.

32. Ibid. 65–85.

33. Forde, *On Being a Theologian of the Cross,* 54.

34. Harold Bloom, *The American Religion: The Emergence of the Post-Christian Nation* (New York: Simon & Schuster, 1992), 59–75.

35. Ibid., 49–51.

36. Horney, *Neurosis,* 37.

37. *LW* 43:177.

38. Irenaeus of Lyons, *Against Heresies,* 4, 20, 7.

CHAPTER 3

1. *LW* 25:441.

2. Merton, *New Seeds of Contemplation,* 99.

3. Robert J. Furey, *So I'm Not Perfect: A Psychology of Humility* (New York: Alba House, 1986), 41.

4. Thinkexist.com, *http://www.thinkexist.com/quotes/golda_meir. html* (accessed May 27, 2008).

5. *LW* 33:62.

6. Forde, *On Being a Theologian of the Cross,* 63.

7. *LW* 43:177.

8. *LW* 25:441.

9. Dag Hammarsköld, *Markings,* trans. Lief Sjoberg and W. H. Auden (New York: Alfred A. Knopf, 1964), 174.

10. *The Shakers: Two Centuries of Spiritual Reflection,* ed. Robley Edward Whitson (New York: Paulist Press, 1983), 294.

11. Thomas Merton, *No Man Is an Island* (New York: Harcourt, 1955), 113–14.

12. Hammarskjöld, *Markings,* 174.

13. Warren Bennis, *On Becoming a Leader* (Cambridge, Mass.: Perseus Publishing, 2003), 40.

14. Jim Collins, *Good to Great* (New York: HarperCollins, 2001), 17–40.

15. Lao Tzu, *Tao Te Ching,* trans. Stephen Mitchell (New York: HarperCollins, 1988), 17.

16. Robert F. Morneau, *Humility* (Winona, Minn.: Saint Mary's Press, 1997), 56.

17. Martin Luther, *Martin Luther's Basic Theological Writings,* 2nd ed., ed. Timothy F. Lull and William R. Russell (Minneapolis: Fortress, 2005), 9.

CHAPTER 4

1. Blumhardt, *Action in Waiting,* 62.

2. Collins, *Good to Great,* 42.

3. Flannery O'Connor, *The Complete Stories* (New York: Noonday Press, 1997), 367.

4. Chuang Tzu, *The Inner Chapters,* trans. David Hinton (Washington, D.C.: Counterpoint, 1997), 105.

5. Anne Wilson Schaef, *When Society Becomes an Addict* (San Francisco: Harper & Row, 1987).

6. Neil Postman, *Technopoply: The Surrender of Culture to Technology* (New York: Vintage Books, 1992), 14.

7. Bonhoeffer, *Life Together*, trans. Bloesch and Burtness, 37.

8. Collins, *Good to Great,* 41–64.

9. Ibid., 46.

10. Samuel Terrien, *The Elusive Presence: The Heart of Biblical Theology* (San Francisco: Harper & Row, 1978), 119–161.

11. John C. Maxwell, *The 21 Irrefutable Laws of Leadership* (Nashville: Thomas Nelson, 2007), 169.

12. Robert Kolb, "Luther on the Theology of the Cross," *Lutheran Quarterly* 16 (2002): 44.

13. Forde, *On Being a Theologian of the Cross*, 80.

14. Wilfrid R. Bion, *Experiences in Groups* (New York: Routledge, 1961), 56, 148.

15. Wengert, "Peace, Peace . . . Cross, Cross," 198.

16. Ibid.

17. *LC* 1, 1–21, in *BC*, 386–388.

18. Ibid.

19. Ibid.

20. Parker J. Palmer, *Let Your Life Speak* (San Francisco: Jossey-Bass, 2004), 4.

CHAPTER 5

1. JSTOR: *Journal for the Scientific Study of Religion* 9, no. 2 (summer 1970) in *http://www.jstor.org/pss/1384984.html* (accessed 5/28/08).

2. Margaret J. Wheatley and Myron Kellner-Rogers, *A Simpler Way* (San Francisco: Berrett-Koehler Publishers, 1996), 68.

3. J. Heinrich Arnold, *Discipleship: Living for Christ in the Daily Grind* (Farmington, Pa.: Plough Publishing House, 1994), 137.

4. *The Essential Rumi*, trans. Coleman Barks (San Francisco: HarperCollins, 1995), 201–202.

5. Collins, *Good to Great*, 65–90.

6. Ibid., 65.

7. Ibid., 85.

8. Rainer Maria Rilke, *Letters to a Young Poet*, trans. Stephen Mitchell (New York: Random House, 1986), 67–68.

9. Wheatley and Kellner-Rogers, *A Simpler Way*, 68.

10. Forde, *On Being a Theologian of the Cross*, 81.

11. *LW* 33:62.

12. Ibid.

13. Forde, *On Being a Theologian of the Cross*, 30.

14. Luther, "On the Councils and the Church, 1539," ed. Lull and Russell, 362–383.

15. Alan Lewis, *Between Cross and Resurrection: A Theology of Holy Saturday* (Grand Rapids: Eerdmans, 2001).

16. *SC* 4, in *BC* 319.

17. Bion, *Experiences in Groups*, 141–190.

18. Ibid.

19. Henri J. M. Nouwen, *Bread for the Journey: A Daybook of Wisdom and Faith* (New York: HarperCollins, 1997), October 18.

20. Gustaf Wingren, *Luther on Vocation*, trans. Carl C. Rasmussen (Eugene, Ore.: Wipf & Stock, 1957), 10–14.

21. Robert Kolb, "The Doctrine of Ministry in Martin Luther and the Lutheran Confessions," in *Called and Ordained*, ed. Todd Nichol and Marc Kolden (Minneapolis: Fortress, 1990), 60.

CHAPTER 6

1. Martin Luther, *The 1529 Holy Week and Easter Sermons*, 94.

2. *The Penguin Dictionary of Epigrams*, 220.

3. Thinkexist.com, in *http://en.www.thinkexist.com/quotes/edith_wharton.html* (accessed May 29, 2008).

4. *I Heard God Laughing: Poems of Hope and Joy by Hafiz*, trans. Daniel Ladinsky (New York: Penguin Books, 2006), 65.

5. Barry Sanders, *Sudden Glory: Laughter as Subversive History* (Boston: Beacon, 1995), 14.

6. Reinhold Niebuhr, "Humour and Faith," in *Discerning the Signs of the Times* (New York: Charles Scribner's Sons, 1949), 111–131.

7. *LW* 54:421.

8. Mark Twain, *The Adventures of Tom Sawyer* (New York: Penguin, 2006), 45.

9. Sanders, *Sudden Glory*, 1.

10. *CD* III/4, 565, 665.

11. Ibid., 565–685.

12. Karl Barth, *Ethics*, trans. Geoffrey W. Bromiley (New York: Seabury, 1981), 511.

13. Ibid.

14. Ibid.

15. Ibid.

16. Ibid.

17. *The Portable Voltaire*, ed. Ben Ray Redman (New York: Viking, 1968), 72–73; Feast of the Ass, *http://www.en.wikipedia.org/wiki/Feast_of_the_Ass.html* (accessed March 13, 2008).

18. "An Evening with Groucho," *http://www.ibras.dk/comedy/marx.html* (accessed Oct. 25, 2007).

19. Niebuhr, "Humour and Faith," 115.

20. *The Best Cartoons from Leadership Journal*, vol. 1 (Nashville: Broadman & Holman, 1999), 46.

21. George Carlin, *Napalm and Silly Putty* (New York: Hyperion, 2001), 102.

22. *Reader's Digest: Laughter, the Best Medicine* (Pleasantville: The Reader's Digest Association, Inc., 1997), 80.

23. James Taylor, *A Porcine History of Philosophy and Religion* (Nashville: Abingdon, 1972).

24. Richard Foster, *Celebration of Discipline*, DVD (Worcester, Pa.: Gateway Films, 1987).

25. Sigmund Freud, "Humour (1928)," in *Character and Culture*, ed. Philip Rieff (New York: Collier Books, 1963), 263–269.

26. Donald Capps, *Laughter Ever After . . . Ministry of Good Humor* (St. Louis: Chalice Press, 2008), 1–121.

27. Catherine Whitmire, ed., *Plain Living: A Quaker Path to Simplicity* (Notre Dame, Ind.: Sorin Books), 20.

SELECT AND ANNOTATED
BIBLIOGRAPHY

"Of making many books there is no end." Ecclesiastes 12:12

Bion, Wilfrid R. *Experiences in Groups.* New York: Routledge, 1961.

These are Bion's seminal papers reflecting his group therapy work with officers in the British military after World War II. Depicts the tug-of-war between the stated mission of groups and their hidden agendas of dependency, fight/flight, and pairing. The writing is elusive and at times stream-of-consciousness. Best read in conjunction with more recent papers from the Tavistock Institute, Bion's institutional legacy.

Bonhoeffer, Dietrich. *Life Together.* Translated by Daniel W. Bloesch and James H. Burtness. Minneapolis: Fortress, 1996.

Though sometimes decried by seminarians as another book by "a dead German," this is the single most eloquent modern description of the church as an assembly of living people under the Word called together by the Spirit. Inspired by the underground seminary life of pre–World War II Germany.

Capps, Donald. *A Time to Laugh: The Religion of Humor.* New York: Continuum, 2005.

The Princeton professor's assessment of the psychic work done by humor. Particularly strong with regard to the countless nuances of joke-telling. A worthy fleshing out of Freud's seminal concept of "saving on psychic resources."

———. *Laughter Ever After . . . Ministry of Good Humor*. St. Louis: Chalice Press, 2008.

A follow-up to the previous book, with reference to the uses of humor in ministry. Again, encyclopedic in its survey of joke-telling categories.

Collins, Jim. *Good to Great: Why Some Companies Make the Leap . . . And Others Don't*. New York: HarperCollins, 2001.

The key nontheological resource behind my book. Endlessly fascinating, Collins and his Stanford research team challenge virtually every current leadership dogma about the "visionary." Will likely stand the test of time. A follow-up to Collins's other major work, *Built to Last.*

Farson, Richard. *Management of the Absurd: Paradoxes in Leadership*. New York: Touchstone, 1996.

One of the few really fine secular business essays on leadership. Distills years of experience in the corporate world and reveals the unintended consequences of almost everything leaders do. An absolute delight and very counterintuitive.

Forde, Gerhard O. *On Being a Theologian of the Cross: Reflections on Luther's Heidelberg Disputation, 1518*. Grand Rapids: Eerdmans, 1997.

Absolutely must reading for anyone wanting to understand from the inside the explosive impact of theology of the cross on contemporary theology, spirituality, and ministry practice. Its theme: the cross *does itself* to us. Should be read once a year until we die.

———. *Where God Meets Man: Luther's Down-to-Earth Approach to the Gospel*. Minneapolis: Augsburg, 1972.

Forde's earliest book. A delightful and accessible introduction to Luther's mindset, especially his critique of religion as preoccupation with "otherworldly" things.

Freud, Sigmund. "Humour" (1928), in *Character and Culture*, 263–269. Edited by Philip Rieff. New York: Collier Books, 1963.

> In this compact essay, Freud focuses on humor's safety-valve function of "saving on the expenditure of psychic resources." Humor as catharsis is the important theme.

Friend, Howard E. "The Failure to Form Basic Partnerships: Resolving a Dilemma of New Pastorates." *Congregations* (September/October 2002), *http://www.pbs.org/thecongregation/indepth/resolvingdilemma.html* (accessed Dec. 7, 2007).

> The author exposes the problem and costs of contemporary ministers' not investing time and energy in relationship building as a prerequisite for all ministry. From a veteran clergy watcher.

Horney, Karen, M.D. *Neurosis and Human Growth.* New York: W. W. Norton, 1950.

> The summary of Horney's life's work. Lays out clearly her still-applicable thesis of the self's skewed development and our tendency to compensate by moving toward, against, and away from others. Powerful in its analysis of the "inner mandates" by which we live.

Hovda, Robert W. *Strong, Loving, and Wise.* Collegeville, Minn.: Liturgical Press, 1976.

> Originally written as a manual for presiding in liturgy and public worship, it has as much to say about the spirit and the manner of leadership in general. Contains the classic description of the leader as "strong, loving, and wise."

Kolb, Robert. "Luther on the Theology of the Cross." *Lutheran Quarterly* 16 (2002): 443–466.

> An excellent journal article summarizing the basics of theology of the cross, with an emphasis on God as both hidden and revealed.

Kolb, Robert, and Charles P. Arand. *The Genius of Luther's Theology: A Wittenberg Way of Thinking for the Contemporary Church.* Grand Rapids: Baker Academic, 2008.

A very readable summary of Luther's thought that, instead of taking the standard topical approach to his theology, goes to its heart by focusing on God's twofold righteousness (passive and active) as an expression of the core nature of humankind.

Lathrop, Gordon W., and Timothy J. Wengert. *Christian Assembly: Marks of the Church in a Pluralistic Age.* Minneapolis: Fortress, 2004.

Talks given to a conference of bishops by the pre-eminent Lutheran confessional and liturgical historians. A contemporary adaptation for the church in North America of "the marks of the church."

Lewis, Alan E. *Between Cross and Resurrection: A Theology of Holy Saturday.* Grand Rapids: Eerdmans, 2001.

A profound and challenging theological treatise on the cross as the paschal mystery of living "in between the times" on Holy Saturday. Academic, rich, and complex, but rewards the hard work of reading.

Luther, Martin. *The 1529 Holy Week and Easter Sermons of Dr. Martin Luther.* Translated by Irving L. Sandberg. Saint Louis: Concordia, 1999.

Wonderful sermons Luther gave the same year as the publication of his Small Catechism. Particularly good in helping one to understand the difference between Christ's suffering and human suffering.

————. *Martin Luther's Basic Theological Writings,* 2nd ed. Edited by Timothy F. Lull and William R. Russell. Minneapolis: Fortress, 2005.

The best modern one-volume selection of key Luther writings, arranged according to theological and pastoral themes. From the American Edition of Luther's works.

Merton, Thomas. *New Seeds of Contemplation.* New York: New Directions, 1961.

Merton's most mature statement of the battle waged in the human soul between the true self and the false self. A primer of contemplative practice as a means for rediscovery of the God-given true self. Eloquent and serene. Bears repeated reading.

Nichol, Todd, and Marc Kolden, editors. *Called and Ordained: Lutheran Perspectives on the Office of the Ministry.* Minneapolis: Fortress, 1990.

A collection of essays on Christian vocation that includes biblical, historical, confessional, pastoral, and ecumenical perspectives.

Niebuhr, Reinhold. "Humour and Faith," in *Discerning the Signs of the Times,* 111–31. New York: Charles Scribner's Sons, 1949.

The great American social ethicist's "big picture" understanding of the role of humor in theology and faith. Contains a helpful distinction between judgment and mercy in humor.

Nouwen, Henri J. M. "A Spirituality of Waiting." In *The Weavings Reader,* 65–74. Edited by John Mogabgab. Nashville: Upper Room Books, 1993.

The author's seminal essay on vocation. Builds on Vanstone's spirituality of the "passion" in the Christian life. Originally an Advent meditation, this is Nouwen's most succinct statement about embracing what we "suffer" or undergo as the fulfillment of our calling.

———. *Life of the Beloved.* New York: Crossroad, 1992.

The prelude to Nouwen's most important work, *The Return of the Prodigal Son.* Baptismal in its orientation. Challenges contemporary culture's scorekeeping and competitive obsessions.

————. *The Way of the Heart: Desert Spirituality and Contemporary Ministry.* New York: Seabury, 1981.

> A primer on survival in ministry. Less appreciated than Nouwen's other writings, it teaches the ancient wisdom of solitude, silence, and prayer as ministry disciplines. One of my personal favorites.

Palmer, Parker J. *A Hidden Wholeness: The Journey toward an Undivided Life.* San Francisco: Jossey-Bass, 2004.

> An extended and sustained continuation of the next title. Like Merton, Palmer finds the root of vocational discernment in the battle of the true self and false self.

————. *Let Your Life Speak: Listening for the Voice of Vocation.* San Francisco: Jossey-Bass, 2000.

> The best single essay in print on finding your personal calling. Probes deeply the shadow side of the leader's person and how he or she may project this onto people. Describes the voice of vocation as the death of our willfulness.

————. *The Promise of Paradox: A Celebration of the Contradictions in the Christian Life.* Washington, D.C.: Servant Leadership School, 1993.

> A series of talks that looks at how suffering and the cross open us to our true vocation.

Rolheiser, Ronald. *The Holy Longing: The Search for a Christian Spirituality.* New York: Doubleday, 1999.

> Anything but otherworldly, this contemporary spirituality begins with the passion, even erotic human yearning, whose life force is variously channeled into longings that are God-centered and for the sake of social responsibility.

Sanders, Barry. *Sudden Glory: Laughter as Subversive History.* Boston: Beacon, 1995.

> An elegant history of laughter in Western culture. The centerpiece of the author's drive-by survey is the storytelling of

Chaucer's *Canterbury Tales.* Views laughter and humor as primarily a matter of social dissent. Indispensable.

Vanstone, W. H. *The Stature of Waiting.* New York: Morehouse, 1982, 2006.

> The late Anglican spiritual writer's meditation on the "passion" at the heart of the Christian life and ministry. Vanstone strongly influences Henri Nouwen's spirituality of vocation as "receiving the initiatives of others." Key to chapter 1 of this book in my description of leadership and ministry as "action in passion."

Weiser, Conrad W. *Healers: Harmed and Harmful.* Minneapolis: Fortress, 1994.

> Reading this sobering analytical discussion of the structural woundedness of religious professionals is like looking into the mirror and beholding your own narcissism, obsessive compulsivity, or depressed dependency. Read it twice and you will marvel that you haven't done more harm! By one of the pre-eminent clinicians of those in church vocations.

Wengert, Timothy J. *A Formula for Parish Practice.* Grand Rapids: Eerdmans, 2006.

> A rich weaving together of parish practice with the theology of the confessional document often considered to be dry and inaccessible. Makes sixteenth-century disputes come alive in the rough-and-tumble of contemporary congregational life.

————. "'Peace, Peace . . . Cross, Cross': Reflections on How Martin Luther Relates the Theology of the Cross to Suffering." *Theology Today* 59 (July 2002): 190–205.

> The Reformation and confessional historian's very personal witness to the cross in his own life, together with a commentary on Luther's overlooked "Explanations of the Disputes Concerning the Power of Indulgences" (1518). Challenges

the misconception that a theology of the cross in any way "blesses suffering."

Wheatley, Margaret J., and Myron Kellner-Rogers. *A Simpler Way.* San Francisco: Berrett-Koehler, 1996.

A lyrical meditation on the order within the chaos of the universe that serves as an analogy of organizational life. Consolidates Wheatley's more technical *Leadership and the New Science.* Actually makes modern physics and quantum theory accessible.

Wingren, Gustaf. *Luther on Vocation.* Translated by Carl C. Rasmussen. Eugene, Ore.: Wipf & Stock, 1957.

The great Swedish scholar's classic account of Luther's theology of Christian vocation. Challenges the pious notion that God somehow "needs" our vocations. It's the neighbor who does. God's doing just fine.

PERMISSIONS

Unless otherwise noted, all Scripture quotations are from the New Revised Standard Version of the Bible, copyright © 1989, Division of Christian Education of the National Council of the Churches of Christ in the United States of America, and are used by permission.

CHAPTER 3

The excerpt on page 55 is from *Markings* by Dag Hammarskjöld, translated by W. H. Auden & Leif Sjoberg, translation copyright © 1964, copyright renewed 1992 by Alfred A. Knopf, a division of Random House, Inc., and Faber & Faber Ltd. Foreword copyright © 1964 by W. H. Auden, copyright renewed 1992 by Edward Mendelson. Used by permission of Alfred A. Knopf, a division of Random House, Inc.

The Nick Hobart cartoon (page 55) is used by permission of the artist.

The verse appearing on page 57 is excerpted from #17 from *Tao Te Ching* by Lao Tzu, a New English version, with foreword and notes, by Stephen Mitchell. Translation copyright © 1988 by Stephen Mitchell. Reprinted by permission of HarperCollins Publishers.

CHAPTER 5

The Rumi verse on page 79 is excerpted from *The Essential Rumi,* trans. Coleman Barks (San Francisco: HarperCollins, 1995), 201–202.

CHAPTER 6

The Hafiz verse on page 101 is an excerpt from "Laughter," from *I Heard God Laughing: Poems of Hope and Joy by Hafiz,* trans. Daniel Ladinsky (New York: Penguin Books, 2006), 65. Copyright © 2006 by Daniel Ladinsky. Reprinted by permission of Daniel Ladinsky.

The Doug Hall cartoons (pages 106 and 113) are used by permission of the artist.

The Rob Portlock cartoons (pages 111 and 112) are used by permission of Rob Portlock.

The Mary Chambers cartoon (page 112) is used by permission of the artist.

The James Taylor cartoons of the Lutheran, Anglican, Methodist, and Kierkegardian pigs (pages 113 and 114) are reprinted from *The New Porcine History of Philosophy and Religion,* by James Taylor, copyright © 1992 by Abingdon Press, and are used by permission of the publisher.

The James Taylor cartoons of the Presbyterian and Baptist pigs (pages 113 and 114) are used by permission of the artist.

The Karl Barth quotes on pages 105 and 107 are from Barth's *Ethics,* trans. Geoffrey W. Bromiley (New York: Seabury, 1981), 511. These excerpts are reprinted by the kind permission of The Continuum International Publishing Group Ltd.